500

mediterranean dishes

500

mediterranean dishes

the only compendium of mediterranean dishes you'll ever need

Valentina Sforza

SELLERS
PUBLISHING

A Quintet Book

Published by Sellers Publishing, Inc.
161 John Roberts Road, South Portland, Maine 04106
For ordering information:
(800) 625-3386 Toll Free
(207) 772-6814 Fax
Visit our Web site: www.sellerspublishing.com
E-mail: rsp@rsvp.com

ISBN: 978-1-4162-0619-4
Library of Congress Control Number: 2010932864
QTT.FHMD

This book was conceived, designed, and produced by
Quintet Publishing Limited
6 Blundell Street
London N7 9BH
United Kingdom

Food Stylist: Valentina Sforza
Photographer: Ian Garlick
Designer: Rod Teasdale
Art Director: Michael Charles
Editorial Assistants: Carly Beckerman-Boys, Holly Willsher
Managing Editor: Donna Gregory
Publisher: James Tavendale

10 9 8 7 6 5 4 3 2 1

Printed in China by 1010 Printing International Ltd.

contents

introduction

It is a well-known fact that the Mediterranean diet incorporates all the traditional healthy living habits of people from the countries bordering the Mediterranean Sea. It includes lots of vegetables, legumes, whole grains, breads, fruits, nuts, seeds, and olive oil, as well as plenty of fish, poultry, and small amounts of red meat—and, in many countries, wine to drink with food. All food that falls under the general heading of Mediterranean is fresh, unprocessed, unrefined, and usually low in saturated and trans fats. The Mediterranean diet is considered to be one of the healthiest ways of eating, with statistics of heart disease and obesity generally recorded as being much lower in those countries where this sort of regime is followed, when compared to other more northern countries.

Recent news that eating a Mediterranean diet during pregnancy might ward off childhood allergies and asthma just adds to the list of studies suggesting this style of eating has a lot to offer. Living longer and having lower risks of heart disease, cancer, diabetes, and possibly birth defects have all been linked to eating a Mediterranean diet.

Of course, there is no one "Mediterranean" diet. There are twenty-one countries that border the Mediterranean Sea. Diets vary between these countries and also between regions within a country. Many differences in culture, ethnic background, religion, economy, and agricultural production result in different diets. But the common Mediterranean dietary pattern has these characteristics:

• high consumption of fruits, vegetables, bread and other whole grains, potatoes, beans, nuts, and seeds

• olive oil as an important monounsaturated fat source

• dairy products, fish, and poultry consumed in low to moderate amounts, and little red meat

- eggs consumed up to four times a week
- wine consumed in low to moderate amounts

Mediterranean food is not just really good for you, it is also really delicious to eat and pretty to look at. It encompasses the culinary traditions and cultures of all the countries that border the Mediterranean waters. This is convivial food that suits the climate and the pace of life, consisting largely of lots of little dishes made out of tantalizing and delicious local specialties—from grilled fish to delicate filled pastries, tasty stews, and fresh produce combined into salads. This is food that will enliven even the most jaded palate, where the key is always variety to satisfy even the hungriest diner.

This book contains many different recipes from all around the Mediterranean, recipes that are traditional and classical as well as new, innovative ideas, chosen because they taste delicious, are relatively simple to reproduce at home, and look simply wonderful on the table—generally bright and colorful, reminiscent of the warm and welcoming Mediterranean.

basic equipment

pots & pans

A big two-handled pot for making stock or for plenty of boiling water for al dente pasta is a must in Mediterranean cooking, as several dishes in this collection will be much easier to make successfully with a pot that is large enough to cope with big quantities of liquid. A solid-based casserole that is suitable for use both in the oven and on the stovetop is very useful for making stews and casserole dishes.

Mediterranean cooking also features a lot of grilling, so a good-sized cast-iron griddle pan will be useful. For shallow frying or sautéing, a steel skillet and a good-quality nonstick skillet will be very useful. For deep-frying, if you don't own a deep-fat fryer, a deep pan made from metal that is not too heavy works equally well. A heavy steel pan is best kept for cooking at a lower temperature than that required for crisp and golden deep-fried foods. (If the oil is not hot enough, the food will simply soak up the oil and come out greasy.)

mixing bowls, colanders & sieves

A good collection of bowls in several sizes makes cooking much easier, as they can be used to combine ingredients or to hold ingredients while waiting to add them to a recipe. Steel bowls are best, as they are lighter and will not absorb strong flavors from ingredients such as garlic or onions, but glass, china, or plastic also work. When a recipe calls for several different ingredients, it is a good idea to measure them out into small ramekins or little bowls so that they can easily and efficiently be added to the dish.

For washing vegetables or for draining pasta and rice, a big colander, preferably made of metal, is always very useful. I also like to have two sieves, one with a very fine wire mesh for sifting dry ingredients and one with larger holes for straining liquids such as stocks or sauces.

measuring cups, spoons & scales

Many of the recipes in this book are quite easygoing about quantities, suggesting that you add a pinch of this or a handful of that. This is the nature of this style of cuisine. For the best results, however, and especially when making some of these recipes for the first time, it is wise to measure ingredients carefully. Even if you don't own a set of kitchen scales, it is always useful to have a set of measuring spoons for small quantities, a measuring cup for liquids, and a set of measuring cups for solids. Once you have perfected the recipes as they are written, you can adjust the quantities according to your personal preferences and taste.

knives & cutting boards

It is really important to have at least one good-quality, sharp kitchen knife for chopping and slicing. A small knife with a serrated blade is vital for cutting all ingredients that have a high citric acid content, such as tomatoes and all citrus fruit. Because you can't cut directly on your counter, cutting boards are absolutely essential, and because you must cut raw meat, fish, and poultry on a separate board from vegetables, fruit, cheese, and bread, two boards will be required. You will also need a pair of good-quality, sharp kitchen scissors, which will help you enormously to carry out a whole range of different jobs from gutting fish to snipping herbs.

other equipment

If you like, you can prepare couscous in a couscousière, which is like a double boiler with the water or stock in the bottom half and the couscous in the top half, the base of which is covered in small holes to allow the steam from the liquid to permeate the couscous. It has a tightly fitting lid to prevent the steam from leaking out. (Otherwise, couscous can be simply prepared by putting it into a bowl and covering it with hot water or stock, then covering with a lid to leave it to steam and absorb the liquid before fluffing it up with a fork.)

For puréeing and blending, an electric stick blender or an immersion blender, is always very useful. A handheld electric whisk will save a lot of time when whipping cream or beating eggs.

Having a good sharp grater is very important for zesting citrus fruits and grating vegetables and cheese. For juicing, a small hand juicer is also very useful. You will also ne0ed a couple of pairs of tongs for turning food and for moving it around safely, as well as a few heatproof rubber spatulas, a balloon whisk, one or two pastry brushes and at least one heatproof brush, a fish slice, and various spoons—slotted, large metal, and wooden.

basic ingredients

bread, pasta, rice & couscous

Bread, pasta, rice, or couscous form the starch base for many dishes of the Mediterranean. This will vary depending upon the country's cuisine. Breads from North African and Middle Eastern countries, as well as Turkey and Greece, are often flat and unleavened, good for wrapping and tearing. Pasta is eaten all over Italy and also as part of many Middle Eastern dishes, often as well as rice. Rice is also widely eaten in the form of salads, as a risotto or as an accompaniment. Please note that rice used for making risotto needs to be of a different kind than that used for boiling. Risotto rice is much more chalky, and it is this chalkiness that forms the creaminess of the dish when diluted with the stock during the cooking process. Rice as an accompaniment for a meat, fish, or vegetable stew is often cooked by steaming it until tender and fluffy.

Couscous is made from ground wheat that has been turned into semolina and then rolled into tiny little balls. Once dried and hardened, the little balls are reconstituted when required with hot liquid or steam to create soft and fluffy couscous to serve as an accompaniment to a whole host of dishes from North Africa, the Middle East, and Sicily. A larger version of more or less the same thing exists on the Mediterranean island of Sardinia, where it is called fregola.

eggs

Eggs form a central part of many aspects of Mediterranean cuisine, either combined with other ingredients to form a dish in their own right, or as vital ingredients for the creation of other dishes, especially for the many custard-based desserts. Using eggs that are as

freshly laid as possible and also from organically fed, free-range chickens will ensure that they have the best taste.

fruits & vegetables

Fruits and vegetables are absolutely fundamental to the Mediterranean way of eating and enjoying food, as any visit to a local market in any one of the countries in the area will show you. The riot of colors and shapes and sizes, with vegetables, fragrant herbs, and juicy fruits piled high in the market stalls gives you a very good indication of where the priorities lie in terms of local ingredients. A great deal of respect is paid to the seasonality of these products as well as to their provenance.

pulses & dried legumes

Legumes are a highly nutritious food group comprising beans, peas, and lentils. When the seeds of a legume are dried, they are called pulses. Pulses represent one of the most important food categories that have been extensively used as staple foods to cover basic protein and energy needs throughout the history of mankind and are widely used in many combinations throughout the different styles of cooking of the Mediterranean. Many experts hold the view that pulses can contribute to health and well-being, mostly through prevention of coronary heart disease and possibly diabetes. The nutritional value of pulses, which are a fundamental key component of the traditional Mediterranean diet, is frequently under-appreciated, despite the wide range of delicious dishes made using a whole variety of these humble ingredients.

fresh & cured meat

On the whole, in comparison with other eating habits, very little meat is eaten as part of the Mediterranean diet. Often it is grilled or spit-roasted over a scented wood fire to make it taste really special. Cured meat, such as prosciutto or pancetta, is widely used as an ingredient to flavor and enhance other dishes.

fish & seafood

Fish and seafood are hugely enjoyed as part of everyday eating, not just as an occasional treat. Always cooked very simply and briefly to make the most of their amazing freshness, fish and seafood are either eaten on their own or combined with other ingredients such as vegetables, rice, pasta, or couscous.

herbs & spices

In some Mediterranean countries, particularly those along the North African coastline and in the southern regions of Italy, dishes are often spiced up by the addition of chile pepper, traditionally dried chile peppers, or dried chili powder or flakes, often in quite explosive quantities. Many other spices, such as cinnamon, cloves, ginger, cumin, and caraway are also used to give many of these traditional dishes their unique identity. Fresh parsley is an absolutely fundamental herb, as well as fresh cilantro, basil, rosemary, and thyme. Basil is really synonymous with the sunny climate of the Mediterranean and grows happily in these parts to be turned into a deliciously dense green sauce called pistou in the south of France and pesto in Liguria.

stocks

Good stocks form the basis of many important dishes, adding flavor to soups, stews, risotto, and sauces. Vegetable stock is the easiest to make and gives the lightest results.

oils & butter

Butter is used extremely sparingly, and sunflower seed or vegetable oils tend only to be used for deep-frying. Generally speaking, the oil of choice in the Mediterranean diet is olive oil, made by crushing the olives that grow so prolifically here.

The health and therapeutic benefits of olive oil were first mentioned by Hippocrates, the father of medicine, who lived from c.460-370 BCE. For centuries, the people of the Mediterranean recognized the nutritional, cosmetic, and medicinal benefits of olive oil. Olive oil has been used to maintain skin and muscle suppleness, heal abrasions, and soothe the burning and drying effects of sun and water. Recent research has now provided firm proof that a Mediterranean diet, which includes large quantities of olive oil, is not only generally healthy but also can help lower harmful LDL cholesterol. Olive oil contains antioxidants that discourage artery clogging and chronic diseases, including cancer.

cheese

Cheese is not a major ingredient in the Mediterranean cuisine, although mozzarella and small quantities of Parmesan and pecorino (ewe's milk cheeses) are used quite widely, as well as soft creamy ricotta. Overall, dairy products are featured very little.

wine

Wine is as synonymous with the traditions of the Mediterranean way of eating as olive oil, and just as ancient. Most Mediterranean people drink moderate amounts of wine with their meals, and some wine is also used for cooking.

antipasti, tapas & mezethes

The custom of serving a selection of small plates of food to begin a meal, or instead of a meal, is very much a part of the Mediterranean culture. Called mezethes, tapas, or antipasti depending upon the country, many of these dishes use very similar basic ingredients, albeit in very different styles.

hummus

see variations page 45

Hummus is one of the best-known and most popular Middle Eastern dips. Served with fresh or toasted pita bread, hummus makes a great snack or appetizer. Tahini is an important part of the hummus recipe and cannot be replaced; however, it can be omitted, if you like, as in the variation on page 45.

1 (16-oz.) can chickpeas or garbanzo beans	2 cloves garlic, crushed
1/4 cup water or vegetable stock	1/2 tsp. salt
3–5 tbsp. lemon juice (depending on taste)	1–2 tbsp. olive oil
1 1/2 tbsp. tahini	chopped fresh parsley, to garnish

Drain chickpeas, reserving liquid from can. Combine chickpeas, water or stock, lemon juice, tahini, garlic, and salt in blender or food processor. Add 1/4 cup of reserved liquid from chickpeas. Blend for 3–5 minutes on low speed until thoroughly mixed and smooth. Place in serving bowl, and create a shallow well in the center of the hummus. Add olive oil in the well. Garnish with chopped parsley. Serve immediately with warm or toasted pita bread. If preferred, cover and refrigerate until required, and add the final oil and parsley garnish just before serving.

Serves 4–6

tzatziki

see variations page 46

Greek tzatziki, traditionally served as an appetizer, can be left on the table as an accompaniment for other foods throughout the meal. The key to the best tzatziki is the thick creamy texture that allows it to be eaten alone, as a dip, spread, or condiment.

1 tbsp. olive oil
2 tsp. lemon juice
2 cups (16 oz.) thick Greek yogurt
4–10 cloves garlic (or to taste), finely chopped

1 cucumber, peeled and finely diced or coarsely grated
chopped fresh parsley, to garnish

Combine the olive oil and lemon juice in a mixing bowl by whisking gently together. Fold the yogurt into the mixture slowly, making sure it is fully mixed in. Add the garlic, according to taste, and the cucumber. Stir until evenly distributed. Garnish with a little chopped parsley. Serve well chilled.

Serves 4–6

sicilian marinated olives

see variations page 47

This way of flavoring olives is very traditional in Sicily, where it is known as *olive cunsati*. The longer the olives are left in their marinade, the stronger the flavor they will take on, but they can be equally delicious served almost immediately after being dressed. Add a handful of these olives to any dish of cured meats for an easy antipasto.

14 oz. green olives, preserved in brine
2 tbsp. chopped fresh dill
4 cloves garlic, peeled and crushed
15 fresh mint leaves
sea salt

1/4 lb. small inner stalks celery with leaves, chopped
6 tbsp. extra-virgin olive oil
8 tbsp. red wine vinegar
1/2 red chile pepper, seeded and finely chopped

Drain the olives, then put them into a heavy-duty plastic bag and loosely tie closed. Place the bag on a worktop and, with a rolling pin, lightly crush the olives (it is more a matter of cracking them), then transfer the olive pulp out of the bag and into a bowl. Add the dill, garlic, mint, and a pinch of salt, then cover with water. Let soak for a minimum of 1 hour or a maximum of 3 days. Drain, then add the celery, olive oil, and vinegar, and finally the chopped chile. Stir it all together thoroughly and serve, or let stand until required.

Serves 4

eggplant dip with walnuts

see variations page 48

The combination of the walnuts and the stinging sharpness of the vinegar used in this recipe gives this Greek dip, called *melitzanosalata me karythia*, a nice tart taste that goes wonderfully with wedges of pita bread, raw vegetables, and salty cheeses.

4 1/2 lbs. of large eggplant(s)
3 cloves garlic
1/3 cup extra-virgin olive oil
3 tbsp. red wine vinegar

1 tsp. salt
1/2 tsp. freshly ground black pepper
1/2 bunch fresh flat-leaf parsley, finely chopped
7 tbsp. coarsely chopped walnuts

Preheat oven to 375ºF. Remove stem from eggplants, rinse, and pat dry. Place whole eggplants on a cookie sheet and bake for just over an hour. Remove from the oven and cool. As soon as they can be handled, remove skin (it will come off easily by hand) and place the pulp in a fine strainer to drain for about 15 minutes, or until it stops dripping.

Combine eggplant pulp with remaining ingredients in a food processor and process until blended. Alternatively, once the eggplant pulp has drained, chop finely, mash with a fork, and stir in all the other ingredients until well blended, adding the oil and vinegar alternately. Serve chilled or at room temperature.

Serves 4–6

egyptian lentils

see variations page 49

This lovely dish of lentils comes from Egypt originally (where it is known as *kosheree*), but many variations on this basic theme exist all over the Mediterranean, where the humble lentil is highly prized and celebrated in lots of different dishes.

1 cup brown lentils, presoaked
1 1/2 cups long-grain rice
1 cup small macaroni
3 tbsp. olive oil
2 fresh red chile peppers, chopped

1 1/2 cups tomato sauce or puréed canned tomatoes
2 tbsp. red wine vinegar, white wine vinegar, or lemon juice
1 large onion, thinly sliced

Place lentils in a pan and cover generously with cold water (there should be about 2 inches of water lying on top of the lentils). Turn the heat to high, bring to a boil, then turn down the heat and simmer, covered, for 35 minutes or until tender. Drain lentils and transfer to a large bowl. Set aside. Bring 3 cups of water to a boil, add rice, then turn down to simmer for 20 minutes. Fluff cooked rice with a fork, and add to the lentils. Bring a large pot of salted water to a boil, add the macaroni, and cook until tender. Drain and add to the lentils and rice.

Put half the olive oil in a small skillet with the chopped chiles. Fry together for about 2 minutes, then add the tomato sauce and vinegar and stir together for 2 or 3 minutes more. Set aside until required. In another skillet, heat the remaining oil and fry the onions until golden. Garnish the lentil mixture with the onions and pour the tomato and vinegar sauce over the top to serve at once.

Serves 4

stuffed grapevine leaves

see variations page 50

Throughout the Middle East and southern Europe, this dish, known as *dolmathakia*, is a real favorite. Ideally, these are made with the very youngest freshly picked grapevine leaves, although preserved leaves ready for stuffing are widely available. The same stuffing can be used to fill vegetables such as zucchini or tomatoes before baking.

juice of 3 1/2 lemons
2 tsp. sea salt
1 (16-oz.) jar 120–150 grapevine leaves, or
    equivalent fresh leaves or flat-packed
    grapevine leaves in brine
1/2 cup olive oil
2 large scallions, finely chopped

1 lb. zucchini, grated
1/2 eggplant, peeled and grated
2 medium carrots, grated
4 ripe tomatoes, peeled, seeded, and chopped
1 1/2 cups long-grain rice
1 bunch fresh flat-leaf parsley, finely chopped
1 tsp. freshly ground pepper

Bring a large pot of water to a boil and add the juice of 1/2 lemon and 1 teaspoon salt. Carefully unroll the leaves without separating them. (It is not unusual for many of the outer leaves in the jar to be damaged or to tear when handled. Set these aside to use later in the recipe.) Turn off the heat and place leaves in the pot for 3 minutes. Remove leaves gently, put them in a bowl, and cover with cold water.

When cooled, drain in a colander. In a large saucepan, heat olive oil and fry the scallions for about 2–3 minutes. Add the zucchini, eggplant, and carrots, and cook over low heat for 10 minutes. Add the chopped tomatoes and continue to cook for 5 minutes. Remove from heat and let cool for 15 minutes. Add the rice, parsley, remaining salt, and pepper, and mix well.

Gently separate one leaf and place it shiny-side down on a work surface. Cut off stem and discard. Place 1 teaspoon of the filling on the leaf at the point where the stem joined the leaf. Fold up bottom of leaf over filling, then each side inward in parallel folds, and roll up the leaf. The roll should be firm, not tight, as the filling will expand during cooking. Repeat until all the filling has been used.

Put a heatproof plate or thick layer of tightly folded baking parchment on the bottom of a heavy, deep pot. Make sure this is a snug fit. Place the filled grapevine leaves on top, packing them closely together but without squeezing them, seam-side down so they don't unroll during cooking. Layer them until they are all in the pot (2–3 layers are best, but no more than 4 layers). Place several unused leaves over the top. Turn another plate upside down on top of the stuffed leaves and weight it down. Add 2 cups water to the pot and cover with a lid. Bring the water to a gentle boil, add the remaining lemon juice, reduce heat to low, and simmer about 50–70 minutes. Check for doneness; if the rice has cooked, they are done. If not, continue cooking another 10 minutes and check again. Cooking time depends both on the type of pot used and the stovetop element. Serve hot or cold.

Serves 10

middle eastern fritters

see variations page 51

The flavor of these very simple little chickpea fritters, known as *sambusac*, will vary according to the spice mixture you add to your filling.

1 lb. all-purpose flour
1 tsp. sea salt
1 package active dry yeast
4 tbsp. olive oil
1 large onion, chopped
2 cloves garlic, chopped

1 (16-oz.) can chickpeas, drained
mixture of ground spices (cumin, coriander, allspice, cinnamon, chili powder, white pepper, etc.), to taste
1 large bunch fresh cilantro or parsley, chopped
about 4 cups canola or vegetable oil, for frying

Mix the flour, sea salt, and yeast with enough warm water to make a pliable dough. You will need up to 2 cups lukewarm water to achieve the right texture. Knead thoroughly for about 15 minutes. Use some of the olive oil to lightly coat a large bowl, then add the dough, cover with a sheet of oiled plastic wrap or a lightly floured cloth, and leave in a warm place for about an hour. While the dough is rising, fry the onion and garlic with the remaining olive oil until just translucent, then add chickpeas and your chosen spices. Mash together to make a sort of paste. Remove from heat, add chopped cilantro or parsley, season to taste, and set aside. Divide the risen dough into about 15 pieces and flatten each one into a small 6-inch circle. Place a generous tablespoonful of the chickpea mixture into the center of each circle and fold over the edges to make a semicircular parcel. Fry these in canola oil that is 4 inches deep until crisp, flipping over once or twice during the cooking process. Transfer onto paper towel to drain, turn over, and drain again. Serve hot or cold.

Serves 6

gildas

see variations page 52

Gilda means "lollipop" in Spanish, and the classic gilda is this simple assembly of a *guindilla* (a Spanish chile pepper), an anchovy, and an olive. The combination of good-quality pinkish anchovies with smallish, crisp, unwrinkled chiles and a freshly pitted olive produces a sophisticated mouthful.

4 oz. best-quality anchovy fillets marinated in
    olive oil
about 2/3 lb. guindilla (or large chiles), cut into
    smaller pieces if necessary
1/2 lb. pitted green olives

Curl up each anchovy and thread it onto a cocktail pick, along with 2 or 3 chiles and 1 olive. Stack the gildas onto a serving plate and serve immediately.

Makes 12

gibraltarian swiss chard pie

see variations page 53

Torte de acelga is traditionally eaten on Good Friday in Gibraltar, a day on which, according to Catholic tradition, no meat is consumed. It is very similar to other versions of this kind of pie or savory cake enjoyed in other parts of the Mediterranean.

6 bunches fresh Swiss chard
1 (15-oz.) package ready-made pie pastry
oil, for greasing
6 eggs
1 cup soft bread crumbs

1 cup grated cheese of your choice
3 tbsp. chopped fresh flat-leaf parsley
2 tsp. minced garlic
sea salt and freshly ground black pepper

Preheat oven to 300ºF. Remove the stems from the Swiss chard leaves for use in another recipe. Boil the leaves, drain very well, and chop finely. Roll out the pastry and lay it in an oiled 8-inch deep pie pan, reserving enough pastry to top the pie later. Beat the eggs, then add bread crumbs, cheese, parsley, garlic, and seasonings. Add egg mixture to the chopped Swiss chard and mix well. Fill the pastry shell with this "relleno" or filling and cover the pie with the saved pastry, sealing the edges well. Cook in the oven for about 30 minutes or until the pie is crisp and golden on top. Serve hot or cold.

Serves 6–8

falafel

see variations page 54

Falafel is very popular in the Middle East as a fast food. Vendors sell it on the street corners in Cairo and in many other towns and cities. As a main dish, it is served as a sandwich, stuffed into pita bread with lettuce, tomatoes, and tahini. As an appetizer, it is served on a salad, or with hummus and tahini. Falafel is a great favorite among vegetarians.

1 cup dried chickpeas or 1 (16-oz.) can
    chickpeas, drained
2 cloves garlic, chopped
1 large onion, chopped
3 tbsp. chopped fresh flat-leaf parsley
1 tsp. ground coriander

1 tsp. ground cumin
sea salt and freshly ground black pepper to
    taste
2 tbsp. flour
canola or vegetable oil for deep-frying

Place dried chickpeas in a bowl, covering with cold water. Allow to soak overnight. Drain the chickpeas, rinse with fresh water, place in pan with fresh water, and bring to a boil. Allow to boil for 5 minutes, then let simmer over a low heat for about an hour. Drain and allow to cool. (Omit these steps if using canned chickpeas.) Combine drained chickpeas, garlic, onion, parsley, coriander, cumin, salt, and pepper in medium bowl. Add flour. Mash chickpeas, combining all ingredients together into a thick paste. (You can also combine ingredients in a food processor.) Form the mixture into small balls, about the size of ping-pong balls. Slightly flatten. Fry in 2 inches of canola oil over medium to high heat until golden brown (5–7 minutes). Drain thoroughly on paper towels and serve hot.

Serves 4

artichoke & manchego rice cakes

see variations page 55

These unusual little croquettes contain artichoke in the rice mixture, and break open to reveal a melting cheese center. Manchego is made from sheep's milk and has a tart flavor that goes wonderfully with the delicate taste of the rice and artichokes.

2 large globe artichokes
4 tbsp. butter
1 small onion, finely chopped
1 garlic clove, finely chopped
1/4 lb. (generous 1/2 cup) long-grain rice
2 cups hot chicken stock

2 oz. grated fresh Parmesan cheese
sea salt and freshly ground black pepper
5 oz. Manchego cheese, very finely diced
3–4 tbsp. fine cornmeal
olive oil, for frying
fresh flat-leaf parsley, to garnish

Remove and discard stalks, leaves, and chokes to leave just the heart of each artichoke. Chop finely. Melt the butter in a pan and gently fry the chopped artichoke hearts, onion, and garlic for 5 minutes until softened. Stir in the rice and cook for about 1 minute. Keeping the heat fairly high, gradually add the stock, stirring occasionally until all the liquid has been absorbed and the rice is cooked—this should take about 20 minutes. Season well, then stir in the Parmesan cheese. Season to taste with salt and pepper. Transfer the mixture to a bowl. Let cool, then cover and chill for at least 2 hours. Spoon about 1 tablespoon of the mixture into the palm of one hand, flatten slightly, and place a few pieces of diced Manchego cheese in the center. Shape the rice around the cheese to make a small ball. Flatten slightly, then roll in the cornmeal, shaking off any excess. Repeat with the remaining mixture to make about 12 cakes. Shallow-fry the rice cakes in hot olive oil for 4–5 minutes, until they are crisp and golden brown. Drain on paper towel and serve hot, garnished with flat-leaf parsley.

Serves 6

mushroom, tomato & mozzarella ciabatta

see variations page 56

This is a simple and tasty snack for two or can be cut into small squares and served as part of an antipasto for larger groups.

1 large ciabatta loaf
3 tbsp. extra-virgin olive oil
1 garlic clove, halved
5 fresh ripe tomatoes, chopped

4 tbsp. wild mushrooms preserved in olive oil, drained
6 oz. buffalo mozzarella, torn into pieces
1/4 lb. fresh arugula
sea salt and freshly ground black pepper

Preheat the broiler. Using a sharp knife, split the ciabatta in half, then cut each half in half again, lengthwise, to give 4 bases. Brush with a little olive oil. Slide under the broiler for 2 minutes until lightly toasted, then rub with the garlic while still warm. Sprinkle the bases evenly with the tomatoes. Top each with some of the mushrooms (halved or quartered if large) and scatter the mozzarella on top. Season, then broil for 2–3 minutes until lightly golden and bubbling. Top with arugula leaves, then drizzle with a little more olive oil to serve.

Serves 2

grilled asparagus wrapped in jamón serrano

see variations page 57

Jamón Serrano is a dry-cured ham, rather like prosciutto. The combination of the slightly metallic flavor of the asparagus and the sweet saltiness of the ham makes for a deliciously tantalizing plateful.

12 medium-thick asparagus, trimmed and
    washed
2 tbsp. extra-virgin olive oil

12 thin slices jamón Serrano
freshly ground black pepper

Preheat a griddle pan until piping hot or preheat the oven to 350°F. Brush the asparagus very lightly with olive oil. Wrap each asparagus stem in the ham and oil lightly on the outside, then cook on the griddle pan or on a cookie sheet in the oven until the edges of the ham are lightly colored and the asparagus is tender enough to be pierced easily with the tip of a knife. Remove from the pan and arrange on a plate. Sprinkle with a little more oil and black pepper and serve.

Serves 4

grilled zucchini with pesto

see variations page 58

The slightly smoky flavor of the grilled zucchini is perfect with the freshness of the pesto, the piquancy of the garlic, and the lovely fresh intensity of the fresh basil.

12 medium-sized zucchini, ends trimmed
1 1/4 cups extra-virgin olive oil
2 cloves garlic, lightly crushed
2 large handfuls fresh basil leaves

2 tbsp. pine nuts
sea salt and freshly ground black pepper
fresh basil leaves to garnish

Slice the zucchini lengthwise into 1/4-inch-thick, long strips. Sprinkle the slices with salt and place them in a colander to drain for about an hour. Wash and dry all the slices, then brush with a little of the olive oil and grill in a griddle pan, under the broiler, or on the barbecue until softened and slightly charred.

Meanwhile, make the pesto by pounding the garlic, basil leaves, and pine nuts together in a mortar and pestle, gradually adding the remaining oil until the right texture has been reached. Alternatively, you can mix everything together in a food processor. Arrange the grilled zucchini on a platter, spoon the pesto on top, garnish with the basil leaves, and serve at once.

Serves 6

antipasti, tapas & mezethes   43

deep-fried stuffed giant olives

see variations page 59

Along the sunny Adriatic coastline of the Marche, these deliciously addictive little mouthfuls are called *olive all'Ascolana*, named after the town of Ascoli Piceno.

60 giant (queen) green olives preserved in brine
1/4 lb. pork fat
1/4 cup extra-virgin olive oil
5 1/2 oz. ground pork
1/4 lb. ground beef
1 tbsp. tomato paste, diluted in a little cold water
3 chicken livers, chopped
3 tbsp. soft white bread crumbs
3 tbsp. beef stock

1 egg, beaten
1 3/4 oz. Parmesan, grated
pinch grated nutmeg
sea salt and freshly ground black pepper
5 tbsp. all-purpose flour
2 eggs beaten with a splash of milk
3–4 tbsp. fine dry bread crumbs
oil for deep frying
lemon wedges, to garnish

Pit all the olives carefully with an appropriate instrument to keep them whole and as neat as possible. Set aside. Fry the pork fat with the oil and the ground pork and beef until the meat is well browned, then add the tomato paste. Mix together and cook for about 20 minutes, then add the chicken livers and cook for another 10 minutes. Cool and chop finely with a heavy knife, or put mixture into a food processor and process until smooth. Add the soft bread crumbs, stock, beaten egg, and Parmesan. Season to taste with nutmeg, salt, and pepper. Carefully fill each olive with this mixture. Roll the olives in flour, then in beaten egg and milk, and then in bread crumbs. Deep-fry in piping hot oil until golden brown, drain on paper towel, and serve hot or cold with the lemon wedges.

Serves 8–10

variations

hummus

see base recipe page 21

hummus without tahini
Prepare basic recipe, omitting tahini. When the hummus is smooth and
creamy, add 1 teaspoon ground cumin.

artichoke hummus
Instead of the basic recipe, combine chickpeas, tahini, and 1 (14-oz.) drained
can of artichoke hearts in food processor. Slowly blend in lemon juice, garlic,
and olive oil. If it is too thick, gradually add water or vegetable stock. Season
with salt and pepper.

roasted garlic hummus
Instead of basic recipe, mix chickpeas, water or stock, lemon juice, and salt
in blender or food processor. Add about 6 cloves of roasted garlic, olive oil,
and 1/2 teaspoon dried oregano. Add extra olive oil, 1/2 teaspoon at a time,
if the hummus is too thick.

kalamata olive hummus
Prepare basic recipe, adding a handful of chopped, pitted Kalamata olives
and a large pinch of dried oregano to the finished hummus, using processor
if desired. Omit parsley garnish.

variations

tzatziki

see base recipe page 22

tzatziki with mint
Prepare the basic recipe, adding about 3 tablespoons finely chopped fresh mint leaves to the mixture with the cucumber.

tzatziki with dill
Prepare the basic recipe, adding about 3 tablespoons finely chopped fresh dill to the mixture with the cucumber.

very quick tzatziki
Instead of the basic recipe, wash and peel 2 cucumbers, then use a vegetable peeler to shave off thin strips of cucumber. Place strips in a colander to drain, sprinkle with salt, and let sit about 10 minutes. Rinse well. Mix strips in a bowl with finely minced fresh garlic, lots of fresh dill, and plain yogurt.

tzatziki with chile
Prepare the basic recipe, adding 1/4 teaspoon finely chopped dried red chile to the mixture with the cucumber for a little added spice.

tzatziki with roasted garlic
Prepare the basic recipe, adding gently roasted, peeled garlic cloves instead of fresh garlic for a softer, sweeter flavor.

sicilian marinated olives

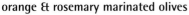
see base recipe page 25

orange & rosemary marinated olives
Drain and rinse a jar of black olives preserved in brine. Mix with juice of 1 large orange, 2 tablespoons chopped fresh rosemary, and olive oil to cover. Let stand until required.

chile & garlic marinated olives
Drain and rinse a jar of black or green olives preserved in brine. Mix with 2–4 chopped dried red chiles, 2–3 crushed garlic cloves, and olive oil to cover. Let stand until required.

lemon & feta marinated olives
Drain and rinse a jar of green or black olives in brine. Mix with juice of 1 lemon; thinly peeled skin of lemon, chopped finely; 2 tablespoons chopped parsley; 2 tablespoons crumbled feta; and olive oil to cover. Let stand until required.

lemon & cilantro marinated olives
Drain and rinse a jar of green olives in brine. Mix with the juice of 1 large lemon, 3 tablespoons chopped cilantro, and olive oil to cover. Let stand until required.

variations

eggplant dip with walnuts

see base recipe page 26

eggplant dip with almonds
Prepare the basic recipe, but replace the walnuts with blanched almonds. Halve
the amount of vinegar.

eggplant dip with pine nuts
Prepare the basic recipe, but replace the walnuts with pine nuts and halve the
amount of vinegar.

eggplant dip with lemon juice
Prepare the basic recipe, but omit the walnuts and replace the vinegar with
1 1/2 tablespoons fresh lemon juice.

eggplant dip with chile
Prepare the basic recipe, but halve the amount of vinegar and stir in 1 finely
chopped fresh red or green chile to the finished dip.

eggplant dip with cilantro
Prepare the basic recipe, but halve the amount of vinegar and omit the walnuts.
Instead, stir about 4 tablespoons finely chopped cilantro into the finished dip.

egyptian lentils

see base recipe page 28

egyptian lentils without pasta
Prepare the basic recipe, omitting the macaroni and adding an extra cup of rice.

mild egyptian lentils
Prepare the basic recipe, omitting the chile peppers for a less spicy dish.

egyptian lentils with mixed herbs
Prepare the basic recipe, stirring in 2 tablespoons mixed chopped fresh herbs before garnishing with the fried onions.

variations

stuffed grapevine leaves

see base recipe page 30

stuffed grapevine leaves with ground chicken
Prepare the basic recipe, replacing the grated eggplant with 4 tablespoons ground chicken.

stuffed grapevine leaves with sausage
Prepare the basic recipe, replacing the carrots with 4 tablespoons skinned and finely chopped pork sausage.

stuffed grapevine leaves with mint
Prepare the basic recipe, replacing the parsley with chopped fresh mint.

stuffed grapevine leaves with lentils
Prepare the basic recipe, replacing the rice with cooked lentils.

variations

middle eastern fritters

see base recipe page 32

middle eastern fritters with lentils
Follow the basic recipe, replacing the chickpeas with canned lentils.

middle eastern fritters with cranberry beans
Follow the basic recipe, replacing the chickpeas with canned cranberry beans.

middle eastern fritters with chile peppers
Follow the basic recipe, adding 2 dried red chile peppers to the onion and garlic. Fry together gently until the onion and garlic are cooked, then discard the chile peppers and continue with the rest of the recipe.

variations

gildas

see base recipe page 35

black olive gildas
Prepare the basic recipe, replacing the green olives with pitted black olives.

caper berry gildas
Thread a caper berry onto the cocktail pick along with the other ingredients.

mild gildas
Omit the chile and simply alternate olives and anchovies on the pick.

gibraltarian swiss chard pie

see base recipe page 36

spinach pie
Prepare the basic recipe, replacing the Swiss chard with about 3 pounds fresh spinach.

asparagus pie
Prepare the basic recipe, replacing the Swiss chard with about 1 pound fresh asparagus.

artichoke pie
Prepare the basic recipe, replacing the Swiss chard with about 12 fresh artichoke bases, quartered.

pea pie
Prepare the basic recipe, replacing the Swiss chard with about 1 1/2 pounds peas.

variations

falafel

see base recipe page 37

falafel with beans
Prepare basic recipe, replacing chickpeas with cannellini or navy beans.

falafel with lentils
Prepare basic recipe, replacing chickpeas with lentils.

chili-flavored falafel
Prepare basic recipe, adding 1 teaspoon chili powder with the
other spices.

falafal with lemon
Prepare basic recipe, replacing the spices with 2 teaspoons finely grated
lemon zest for a different kind of flavor.

variations

artichoke & manchego rice cakes

see base recipe page 38

artichoke & mozzarella rice cakes
Prepare the basic recipe, replacing the Manchego with mozzarella for a milder-tasting rice cake.

artichoke & scamorza rice cakes
Prepare the basic recipe, replacing the Manchego with smoked Scamorza (matured mozzarella) for a much more complex taste.

asparagus rice cakes
Prepare the basic recipe, replacing artichokes with about 10 chunky asparagus, chopped.

variations

mushroom, tomato & mozzarella ciabatta

see base recipe page 40

mushroom, tomato & smoked scamorza ciabatta
Prepare the basic recipe, replacing mozzarella with slices of smoked
Scamorza for a much stronger flavor.

sun-dried tomato, fresh tomato & mozzarella ciabatta
Prepare the basic recipe, replacing mushrooms with marinated
sun-dried tomatoes.

fresh tomato, pesto & mozzarella ciabatta
Prepare the basic recipe, omitting the mushrooms and spreading the garlic-
rubbed ciabatta with a thin layer of pesto before adding the tomatoes and
the mozzarella and broiling.

variations

grilled asparagus wrapped in jamón serrano

see base recipe page 41

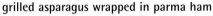

grilled asparagus wrapped in parma ham
Prepare the basic recipe, replacing the Serrano ham with slices of Parma ham.

grilled asparagus with jamón serrano & manchego
Prepare the basic recipe, sprinkling the finished dish with a few shavings of Manchego cheese.

grilled asparagus with jamón serrano & mozzarella
Prepare the basic recipe, but line the slices of ham with thin strips of mozzarella before wrapping the asparagus.

grilled asparagus with jamón serrano & parmesan
Prepare the basic recipe, covering the wrapped asparagus with freshly grated Parmesan before grilling or baking. Cook until the cheese becomes golden and slightly crisp.

variations

grilled zucchini with pesto

see base recipe page 43

grilled peppers with pesto
Prepare the basic recipe, replacing the zucchini with 6 quartered and seeded bell peppers. Omit the salting step.

grilled eggplant with pesto
Prepare the basic recipe, replacing the zucchini with 4 large eggplant, sliced lengthwise into 1/4-inch-thick slices.

grilled zucchini with mint & parsley pesto
Prepare the basic recipe, replacing the basil in the pesto with mint and parsley and omitting the garlic.

grilled zucchini with almond pesto
Prepare the basic recipe, replacing the pine nuts in the pesto with almonds.

variations

deep-fried stuffed giant olives

see base recipe page 44

deep-fried stuffed giant olives with chicken
Prepare the basic recipe, replacing the ground pork and beef with the same
amount of ground chicken.

deep-fried stuffed giant olives with turkey
Prepare the basic recipe, replacing the ground pork and beef with the same
amount of ground turkey.

deep-fried stuffed giant olives with lemon zest
Prepare the basic recipe, but omit the chicken livers and nutmeg and add
2 teaspoons finely grated lemon zest.

soups

Mediterranean soups are a popular way to start the meal, especially in bad weather or when fall evenings start to feel chilly. Some Mediterranean soups can be a meal in themselves, with plenty of nourishing beans, which makes them really filling.

gazpacho

see variations page 79

This refreshing cold soup originated in Andalusia in Spain, where it is nicknamed *Andalusian liquid salad*. Cold soup is ideal for the summer months and occasions such as barbecues, and gazpacho is an ideal healthy starter because of the high proportion of vegetable ingredients. It is easily made and can be prepared hours prior to serving and stored in the fridge.

1 red bell pepper
1 green bell pepper
1 cucumber, peeled, halved, and seeded
1/2 onion
1 clove garlic, crushed
6 ripe tomatoes, seeded
1 (14-oz.) can chopped tomatoes

3/4 cup extra-virgin olive oil
4 tbsp. red wine vinegar
salt and freshly ground black pepper
1/4 cucumber, peeled, seeded, and chopped
chopped fresh chives, for garnish
4 warmed crispy rolls, to serve

Blanch the peppers in boiling water for about 2 minutes to loosen the skin, then peel, remove the seeds, and core. Dice half of each pepper and half the cucumber and set aside. Put the other pepper halves, onion, remaining cucumber, garlic, fresh and canned tomatoes, olive oil, and red wine vinegar into a blender or food processor and blend until a smooth liquid. Season with salt and pepper. Pour the liquid into a large bowl and refrigerate for at least 1 hour. Just as you are about to serve the soup, ladle portions into chilled bowls. Add the remaining chopped red and green pepper and chopped cucumber to each bowl. Garnish with the chopped chives and serve with the warm rolls.

Serves 4

warm fish soup on a bed of toasted garlic bread

see variations page 80

This is the easiest recipe for making a really Mediterranean-tasting fish soup. You can add mussels, shrimp, and all manner of other fish or seafood if you wish, although the basic recipe calls only for filleted white fish, which makes it really easy to eat. The bread soaks up all the flavors and juices of the fish and is eaten at the end, once all the fish has gone.

3 lbs. (approximately) filleted fish of various
    kinds (e.g., cod, monkfish, haddock, plaice)
8 tbsp. olive oil
5 cloves garlic, finely chopped
1 dried red chile pepper
6 tbsp. chopped fresh flat-leaf parsley
3 handfuls cherry tomatoes, halved

sea salt and freshly ground black pepper
1 1/4 cups dry white wine
1 cup fish stock
12 thin slices ciabatta bread, toasted
1 clove garlic, peeled and left whole
2 tbsp. extra-virgin olive oil, to serve

Trim all the fish fillets carefully, cut them into equal-sized chunks, wash, and pat dry. Heat the oil in a deep saucepan with the garlic, chile, 4 tablespoons of parsley, and tomatoes for about 5 minutes. Add all the fish and stir. Season with salt and pepper and add the wine and fish stock. Cover tightly and simmer very gently for about 15 minutes. Meanwhile, toast the bread slices, rub each side with the garlic, and line a large, wide serving bowl with the bread. Pour the hot fish soup all over the bread, drizzle with a little olive oil, sprinkle with the remaining parsley, and serve at once.

Serves 6

avgolemono

see variations page 81

This classic and flavorful soup recipe originated in Greece and combines eggs and lemon with rice and chicken stock to create a lovely zesty taste.

2 cups milk
2 tbsp. cornstarch
6 egg yolks, beaten
2 quarts chicken stock
1/2 cup long-grain rice

1/4 cup butter
2 tbsp. chopped fresh flat-leaf parsley
1/2 cup fresh lemon juice (or more to taste)
finely grated zest of 1 lemon
salt and freshly ground black pepper

Stir the milk and cornstarch together until smooth. Beat in the egg yolks. Set aside.

Bring the stock to a boil in a large pot, and add the rice. Cook, covered, over low heat until the rice is puffy and tender, about 25 minutes. Remove the soup from heat, and add the milk and egg mixture very gradually, stirring constantly to prevent lumps forming. Put the soup back on the burner and continue to cook for a moment, stirring, until it thickens. Remove from the heat again and add the butter, chopped parsley, lemon juice, and finely grated lemon zest. Season to taste with salt and pepper, stir once more, and serve immediately.

Serves 10

lebanese mixed bean soup

see variations page 82

This wonderfully filling and nourishing soup is called *makhluta* in Lebanese and uses just about every kind of bean available! To save time, you can use canned beans instead of the dried, which means you can eliminate the overnight soaking step.

1/2 cup dried white kidney beans
1/2 cup dried red beans
1/2 cup dried chickpeas
1/4 cup dried black fava beans
1/4 cup dried big black lentils
2 quarts water
1 tbsp. vegetable oil

2 medium onions, finely chopped
1/4 cup coarse bulgur
1/4 cup short-grain rice
1/2 tsp. ground cumin
1 tsp. salt
4 tbsp. lemon juice
1 lemon, cut into wedges, to serve

Soak kidney beans, red beans, and chickpeas in water for 12 hours. Soak the fava beans separately in water for 12 hours. Drain the beans. Put kidney beans, red beans, and chickpeas in a large pan. Add the lentils. Cover with the 2 quarts of water, set pan over high heat, and bring to a boil. Lower heat and cook for 30 more minutes. Cook fava beans separately using the same method, but after cooking for 30 minutes, drain and discard the cooking liquid. Add drained fava beans to the other beans.

In a large stockpot, heat oil, add onions, and stir-fry until browned. Add the beans with the bulgur, rice, cumin, and salt. Cook over low heat, stirring occasionally, for 30 minutes or until rice is tender. Add lemon juice and cook over low heat for 5 more minutes. Serve hot, with lemon wedges.

Serves 6

moroccan chickpea soup

see variations page 83

This delicious soup looks wonderfully colorful and has a lovely citrus flavor that really brings it to life.

1 tbsp. extra-virgin olive oil
1 medium onion, chopped
2 celery stalks, chopped
2 tsp. ground cumin
2 1/2 cups hot vegetable stock
1 (14-oz.) can chopped canned tomatoes
1 (14-oz.) can chickpeas, rinsed and drained

freshly ground black pepper
1/4 lb. frozen or fresh fava beans
zest and juice of 1/2 lemon
1/4 tsp. sea salt
large handful fresh cilantro, chopped
flatbread, to serve

Heat the oil in a large saucepan, then fry the onion and celery gently for 10 minutes until softened, stirring frequently. Add the cumin and fry for another minute. Turn up the heat and add the stock, tomatoes, and chickpeas, plus a good grinding of black pepper. Simmer for 8 minutes. Add fava beans and lemon juice and cook for 2 minutes more. Season to taste, then top with a sprinkling of lemon zest and chopped cilantro. Serve with flatbread.

Serves 4–6

provençal soup

see variations page 84

This very simple soup will remind you of the lazy hazy south of France—healthy, tasty, colorful—the simple pleasures of life in the sunshine! Serve with toasted rustic or farmhouse bread.

3 large potatoes
3 large tomatoes
about 1 1/2 quarts cold water
sea salt and freshly ground black pepper
2 tbsp. olive oil
2 onions, finely chopped

1 clove garlic, halved
4 baguette slices, toasted
2 tbsp. dried fines herbes de Provence (or a combination of tarragon, parsley, and chervil)

Peel potatoes and cut them in half. Blanch tomatoes for 15 seconds in boiling water, then drain, cool, and peel. Cut them in half and remove seeds. Put potatoes and tomatoes in a large saucepan filled with the cold water. Season with salt and pepper and bring to a boil. Lower heat and let simmer, covered, for 1 hour. Heat oil in a skillet on medium heat. Add onions and fry for 20 minutes over low heat, without burning them. Add 1 cup of liquid from the tomatoes and potatoes saucepan and simmer for 15 minutes. Put onion mixture into a blender. Drain potatoes and tomatoes, reserving the liquid. Add them to the blender. Purée, adding as much liquid as necessary from the saucepan to achieve the desired consistency. Season to taste.

Rub garlic halves over the toasted bread slices. Put the slices on the bottom of soup bowls and add the soup. Sprinkle the chopped herbs on the top. Serve very hot.

Serves 4

looz shorba

see variations page 85

Looz shorba is a deliciously rich and creamy almond soup with a wonderfully sweet flavor. Make sure the almonds are really fresh for the best results.

2 tbsp. sweet butter
1/2 cup chopped onions
2 tbsp. all-purpose flour
1 quart boiling chicken stock

1/2 cup ground blanched almonds
1/2 cup heavy cream
sea salt and freshly ground white pepper

Melt the butter in a saucepan, add the onions, and cook until soft but not browned. Stir in the flour. When smooth, add the boiling stock, stirring briskly. Allow to simmer for a few minutes. Stir in the ground almonds. Cook, simmering, for 20 minutes. Stir in the cream and allow to heat through. Season with salt and pepper to taste. Serve hot.

Serves 4

spanish squash & apple soup

see variations page 86

This delicious squash soup, called *crèma de calabaza* in its native Spain, is sharpened by the flavor of the apple, which cleverly takes away some of the dense, sweet flavor of the squash.

1 medium acorn squash, halved and cleaned
1 apple, peeled and roughly chopped
1 large onion, peeled and roughly chopped
1 potato, peeled and roughly chopped
2 carrots, peeled and roughly chopped
1/4 carcass roast chicken (optional)
1 tbsp. Spanish sweet paprika

3 generous cups water
1 tsp. dried oregano
1 cup whole milk
sea salt and freshly ground black pepper to taste
6 slices crusty bread, toasted
1 apple, skin on and thinly sliced

Preheat the oven to 375ºF. Put the halved acorn squash on a cookie sheet and bake for about 1 hour or until softened. While the squash is baking, prepare the vegetables. Put the apple, onion, potato, and carrots in a large pan with the chicken carcass, paprika, water, and oregano. Simmer for about 40 minutes, adding more water if necessary. Remove and discard chicken carcass (if using). Remove the softened squash from the oven and remove skin and any remaining seeds. Put the cooked flesh of the squash into the soup and stir in the milk. In a blender or food processor, purée the soup completely and return to the heat. In a separate pan, soften the slices of apple in boiling water for 5 minutes. Season the soup to taste and serve in a warm soup tureen or individual bowls lined with the toasted bread, with a few of the softened apple slices for each serving.

Serves 6

tomato & basil soup

see variations page 87

This refreshing cold tomato and basil soup makes a perfect lunch dish on a hot summer's day. It goes especially well with crostini and pesto.

1/2 onion, peeled
2 stalks celery, with leaves
1 carrot, peeled and finely diced
4 tbsp. olive oil
1 lb. ripe fresh tomatoes

1 (14-oz.) can plum tomatoes, with liquid
1 quart chicken or vegetable stock
1 large bunch fresh basil
sea salt and freshly ground black pepper

Cut the onion in half and slice sideways. Slice the celery into thin half-moons. Place a large pan over low heat and add the oil. Heat gently and add the onions, carrots, and celery. Stir well. Cook gently until soft. Core tomatoes, halve, and dice into chunks. Add chunks to the pan, and cook for a few minutes. Add the canned tomatoes and stir. Add just enough stock to cover, and stir again. Bring to a boil, cover, and turn down the heat to a simmer. Cook for 15–20 minutes.

Strip the leaves from the basil stalks, then tear the leaves in half with your fingers. Add half of the leaves to the soup. Stir, then replace the pan lid, and cook for 10 minutes. Once cooked, remove from the heat and allow the soup to cool for a few minutes before adding the remaining fresh basil. Stir, season with salt and pepper, and stir again. Using a blender, blend the soup on high power for a couple of minutes until it takes on a smooth, velvety texture. If desired, add more stock for a thinner consistency. Chill for 2 hours before serving.

Serves 4–6

summer minestrone

see variations page 88

The word "minestrone" means "big soup," and this soup is certainly a big one, packed with lots of different vegetables, beans, and pasta.

7 oz. borlotti (cranberry) beans, canned or dried
4 tbsp. olive oil
1 onion, finely chopped
handful of fresh flat-leaf parsley, chopped
10 oz. mixed fresh green vegetables (e.g.,
    spinach, cabbage, Swiss chard, lettuce
    leaves), chopped

2 zucchini, cubed
1 potato, peeled and cubed
1 carrot, cubed
sea salt and freshly ground black pepper
7 oz. short stubby pasta
2–3 tbsp. best-quality pesto (page 178)
freshly grated Parmesan cheese, to serve

If using dried beans, soak overnight in cold water, drain, rinse, then boil fast in cold water for 5 minutes. Drain, rinse, and boil in fresh water or stock until tender but not falling apart. Do not add salt to the water until the beans are tender, as this will cause the skin to shrivel and harden. Drain beans, reserving cooking liquid. Fry onion gently in the olive oil until soft. Add cooked (or canned and drained) beans and stir together thoroughly. Add parsley, green vegetables, zucchini, potato, and carrot. Fry together gently, using the water from the boiled or canned beans to moisten. When the vegetables are beginning to soften, pour in the rest of the bean water (or in the case of canned beans, add vegetable stock instead) to cover thoroughly, turn the heat down, and simmer slowly for about 30 minutes, stirring regularly. Add more liquid if necessary, using vegetable stock or water. When vegetables are thoroughly soft, season to taste and add pasta. Cook gently until pasta is cooked. Remove from heat, stir in pesto, and transfer into soup bowls or a tureen and serve, sprinkled with a little freshly grated Parmesan.

Serves 6

lebanese red lentil soup

see variations page 89

This is a wonderful recipe from Lebanon that sort of resembles an old-fashioned split-pea soup. Serve garnished with lemon wedges.

1 1/2 quarts chicken stock
1 lb. red lentils
3 tbsp. olive oil
1 tbsp. minced garlic
1 large onion, chopped

1 tbsp. ground cumin
1/2 tsp. cayenne pepper
1/2 cup chopped fresh cilantro
juice of 1/2 lemon
8 lemon wedges, to garnish

Bring chicken stock and lentils to a boil in a large saucepan over high heat, then reduce heat to medium-low, cover, and simmer for 20 minutes.

Meanwhile, heat olive oil in a skillet over medium heat. Stir in garlic and onion, and cook until the onion has softened and turned translucent, about 3 minutes. Stir the garlic and onion into the lentils, and season with cumin and cayenne. Continue simmering until the lentils are tender, about 10 minutes.

Carefully purée the soup in a blender or with a handheld blender until smooth. Stir in cilantro and lemon juice before serving, and garnish each serving with a lemon wedge.

Serves 8

variations

gazpacho

see base recipe page 61

lemony gazpacho
Prepare the basic recipe, adding the juice of 1 lemon to the other ingredients in the food processor. Add a thin slice of lemon to the garnish.

gazpacho with croutons
Prepare the basic recipe, but instead of serving the soup with the warm roll, make some croutons with 3 slices of white bread, cut into cubes and fried in a little oil until crisp and lightly browned. Sprinkle these over each bowl of soup to serve.

gazpacho with almonds
Omit the peppers, onion, cucumber, and tomatoes. Replace them with 1 cup blanched almonds and 2 cups stale white bread (crusts removed), soaked until spongy in cold water and squeezed dry. Add an extra clove of garlic and a generous splash of white wine or sherry vinegar and proceed as above, adding just enough cold water to create a creamy soup consistency. Sprinkle with a few toasted slivered almonds to serve.

gazpacho with lime
Omit the vinegar, and replace it with 4 tablespoons freshly squeezed lime juice for a very different, crisp citrus flavor.

variations

warm fish soup on a bed of toasted garlic bread

see base recipe page 62

warm fish & mussel soup on toasted garlic bread
Prepare the basic recipe, adding a large handful of cleaned fresh mussels to the saucepan, after adding the fish, wine, and fish stock.

warm fish & shrimp soup on toasted garlic bread
Prepare the basic recipe, adding about 10 shelled and deveined shrimp to the saucepan with the fish.

warm fish & squid soup on toasted garlic bread
Prepare the basic recipe, adding 2 or 3 small squid, cleaned and cut into chunks, to the saucepan with the fish fillets.

smooth fish soup on toasted garlic bread
Prepare the basic recipe, but when the fish is cooked, blend or process it to a smooth creamy texture before pouring it over the garlic bread.

avgolemono

see base recipe page 65

avgolemono with basil
Prepare the basic recipe, replacing the parsley with 2 tablespoons finely shredded fresh basil leaves and the finely grated lemon peel with 1 teaspoon pesto (page 178).

vegetarian avgolemono
Prepare the basic recipe, replacing the chicken stock with a richly flavored vegetable stock. Make the stock by gently boiling together even quantities of celery, carrots, and onions with a few parsley stalks in about 2 1/2 quarts of water for about 1 hour. Strain the resulting liquid and season to taste with salt and pepper before using.

avgolemono with shredded chicken
Prepare the basic recipe, but for a more substantial soup, add the finely shredded meat from 2 poached small chicken breasts to the soup with the milk and egg mixture.

avgolemono with chives
For a very slight onion flavor, omit the chopped parsley and replace with the same quantity of finely chopped fresh chives, washed and dried.

variations

lebanese mixed bean soup

see base recipe page 66

lebanese spicy mixed bean soup
Prepare the basic recipe, adding 2 small dried red chile peppers, finely chopped, to the oil and onions before adding the beans and the other ingredients.

lebanese mixed bean soup with garlic
Prepare the basic recipe, replacing the onions with 6 minced garlic cloves.

lebanese mixed bean & tomato soup
Prepare the basic recipe, adding 4 peeled, seeded, and roughly chopped fresh tomatoes to the oil and onions before adding the beans and the other ingredients.

moroccan chickpea soup

see base recipe page 68

moroccan chickpea soup with peas
Prepare the basic recipe, replacing the beans with fresh or frozen peas.

moroccan chickpea soup with parsley
Prepare the basic recipe, replacing the chopped cilantro with the same amount
of flat-leaf parsley.

moroccan chickpea soup with chicken
Prepare the basic recipe, adding 2 small and skinless chicken breasts,
cooked and finely shredded, with the chickpeas to the soup for a much
more substantial dish.

variations

provençal soup

see base recipe page 69

provençal soup with pesto
Prepare the basic recipe, but instead of finishing off the soup with the dried herbs, put 1/2 teaspoon of fresh pesto (page 178) on top of each bowl of soup to serve.

provençal soup with croutons
Prepare the basic recipe, but instead of putting the garlicky bread slices on the bottom of the bowls, make some croutons with 3 slices of white bread, cut into cubes and fried in a little oil until crisp and lightly browned. Sprinkle these over each bowl of soup to serve.

provençal soup with celery
Prepare the basic recipe, giving some extra flavor to the soup by adding 3 stalks celery, strings removed, to the potatoes and tomatoes. Instead of sprinkling the dried herbs on top of each serving, garnish with 1 finely chopped small celery stalk and a few celery leaves.

variations

looz shorba

see base recipe page 70

almond looz shorba
Prepare the basic recipe, replacing the chicken stock with a richly flavored vegetable stock. Make the stock by gently boiling together even amounts of celery, carrots, and onions with a few parsley stalks for about 1 hour in about 1 1/2 quarts water. Strain the resulting liquid and season to taste with salt and pepper before using.

looz shorba with toasted almonds
Prepare the basic recipe, sprinkling 1 tablespoon dry-roasted slivered almonds over each serving.

almond looz shorba with chicken
Prepare the basic recipe, adding 2 small boneless and skinless chicken breasts, cooked and shredded, to the soup with the cream.

spicy almond looz shorba
Prepare the basic recipe. Stir a tablespoon of hot chilli oil through the soup in a swirl, to serve.

variations

spanish squash & apple soup

see base recipe page 72

spanish squash & pear soup
Prepare the basic recipe, replacing the apple with a large ripe pear.

spanish squash & apple soup with apple purée garnish
Prepare the basic recipe. To add more apple flavor, drop 1 teaspoon unsweetened cooked apple purée or chunky applesauce into the center of each bowl of soup just before serving.

spanish pumpkin & apple soup
Prepare the basic recipe, replacing the squash with a small pumpkin.

spanish squash & apple soup with bacon
Prepare the basic recipe, then finish off the soup with 6 tablespoons crisply fried warm bacon cubes, scattered over the top just before serving.

variations

tomato & basil soup

see base recipe page 75

fresh tomato & basil soup with croutons
Prepare the basic recipe. Serve the cold soup with a scattering of croutons
made from 3 slices of white bread, cut into cubes and fried in a little oil until
crisp and lightly browned.

fresh tomato & basil soup with pesto
Prepare the basic recipe. Finish off each bowl of cold soup by stirring
1/2 teaspoon fresh pesto (page 178) through just before serving.

fresh tomato & basil soup with fried basil leaf garnish
Prepare the basic recipe. To finish off the soup, fry about 12 fresh, washed, and
dried basil leaves in 1/2 inch of oil for about 30 seconds or until just crisp and
translucent. Float these on top of each bowl just before serving.

fresh roasted tomato & basil soup
On a cookie sheet, drizzle olive oil over fresh tomatoes and roast gently in the
oven until soft. Prepare the basic recipe using the roasted tomatoes.

variations

summer minestrone

see base recipe page 76

summer minestrone with rice
Prepare the basic recipe, replacing pasta with 6 ounces of long-grain rice.

cold summer minestrone
Prepare the basic recipe, but allow the soup to cool and thicken before adding the pesto and serving at room temperature.

summer minestrone with chickpeas
Prepare the basic recipe, replacing borlotti beans with dried or canned chickpeas.

summer minestrone with squash or pumpkin
Prepare the basic recipe, replacing the zucchini with the same quantity of peeled, seeded, and cubed winter squash or pumpkin.

variations

lebanese red lentil soup

see base recipe page 78

vegetarian lebanese red lentil soup

Prepare the basic recipe, replacing the chicken stock with a richly flavored vegetable stock. Make the stock by gently boiling together even quantities of celery, carrots, and onions with a few parsley stalks in about 2 quarts of water for about 1 hour. Strain the resulting liquid and season to taste with salt and pepper before using.

lebanese red lentil soup with croutons

Prepare the basic recipe. Make some croutons with 3 slices of brown or white bread, cut into cubes and fried in a little oil until crisp and lightly browned. Sprinkle these over each bowl of soup before serving.

chunky lebanese red lentil soup

Prepare the basic recipe, but do not purée or blend the soup to make it smooth. Instead, serve it with the lentils as they are.

spicy lebanese red lentil soup

Prepare the basic recipe, adding an extra 1/2 teaspoon cayenne pepper or 1 small dried red chile pepper, finely chopped, with the cumin to give the soup extra spicy heat.

salads

In hot weather, imaginative, refreshing, yet nourishing salads are an absolute must. This chapter contains many of the classic salads, as well as some more unusual examples of salads prepared in many of the Mediterranean countries during summer, when fresh produce is at its very best.

roasted eggplant & mint salad

see variations page 112

A really delicious salad using eggplant and mint—a perfect flavor combination—with a little feta cheese to add some creamy saltiness to the finished dish.

1 large eggplant
about 3 tbsp. extra-virgin olive oil
sea salt and freshly ground black pepper
1/3 lb. feta cheese, crumbled

1 small clove garlic, finely chopped
handful fresh mint leaves, shredded
handful fresh cilantro leaves, shredded
squeeze of lemon juice

Preheat the oven to 425°F. Brush the eggplant slices on both sides with oil and season with salt and pepper. Place on a cookie sheet in a single layer. Roast for 15–20 minutes, turning, until golden. Allow to cool to room temperature. Arrange the eggplant slices on a serving plate. Scatter the crumbled feta over the top, along with the garlic, mint, and cilantro. Add a squeeze of lemon juice and serve.

Serves 4

neapolitan roasted pepper salad

see variations page 113

This is such a classic, delicious antipasto and incredibly addictive! Also delicious with mozzarella in a sandwich made with crusty bread.

6 large red and/or yellow bell peppers
3 cloves garlic, very finely chopped
large handful fresh flat-leaf parsley, chopped

8 tbsp. extra-virgin olive oil
sea salt and freshly ground black pepper

Preheat the oven to 400°F. Wash and dry peppers, then lay them on a rack or in a shallow metal pan in the oven for about 30 minutes, or until browned and soft. Remove from oven and lay them in a deep tray on the counter. Cover the peppers with a large glass bowl so that they can steam as they cool, thus loosening their skins. As soon as the peppers are cool enough to handle easily, slip off their thin, papery skins and slide out their seeds.
(Or you can wrap the roasted peppers in plastic wrap until cool, then peel and seed.)

Cut the prepared peppers in to wide slices and arrange, slightly overlapping, on a platter or in a shallow-sided bowl. Sprinkle with the garlic and parsley and then sprinkle with the olive oil and salt and pepper. Mix gently to evenly distribute the seasoning, then let stand for an hour or more to allow the flavors to develop before serving.

Serves 6

salad niçoise

see variations page 114

This classic salad is synonymous with the south of France, combining salad ingredients, herbs, eggs, and olives to make a very pretty and delicious dish topped off with a lightly grilled fresh tuna steak.

3 tbsp. aged red wine vinegar
7 tbsp. extra-virgin olive oil
2 tbsp. chopped fresh flat-leaf parsley
2 tbsp. snipped fresh chives
2 cloves garlic, peeled and finely chopped
1 tsp. sea salt
1 tsp. freshly ground black pepper
1 lb. fresh tuna loin or 4 (6-oz.) tuna steaks, 1 inch thick
4 Little Gem lettuce hearts (or crisp long-leafed lettuce, quartered lengthwise)

1 red onion, finely sliced
4 fresh plum tomatoes, roughly chopped
8 new potatoes, cooked and quartered lengthwise
1/4 lb. extra-fine haricots verts, topped, cooked, and drained
6 anchovy fillets, cut lengthwise into thin strips
4 eggs, cooked for 6 minutes in boiling water from room temperature, halved
16 pitted black olives in brine, drained
8 fresh basil leaves, torn

Whisk together the red wine vinegar, olive oil, parsley, chives, garlic, salt, and pepper. Place the tuna in a shallow dish and cover with half of the dressing. Cover and chill for 1–2 hours to allow the fish to marinate. Toss tuna in the marinade from time to time. Heat a ridged griddle pan under a hot broiler for 5 minutes. Remove the tuna from the marinade and place on the pan. Cook the tuna steaks for 2–3 minutes on each side, depending on how rare you like your fish. Cook the tuna loin (if using) for about 15 minutes or longer, turning frequently. Lay the lettuce leaves on a large plate and add the onion, tomatoes, potatoes, haricots verts, and anchovies. Arrange the cooked tuna on top. Drizzle with the remaining dressing, then finish by adding the halved eggs, olives, and basil leaves.

Serves 4

insalata caprese

see variations page 115

This absolutely classic salad originates from the beautiful island of Capri. It is truly unforgettable when made with the local richly flavored tomatoes, the soft and silky local buffalo mozzarella, and the intensely perfumed basil grown on the volcanic terrain. It is a lesson in the use of very few but perfect ingredients put together with simple skill.

2 handfuls (i.e. 2 very large, or 4 medium-sized, or 12 cherry tomatoes, or a mixture) firm ripe tomatoes, washed well
2 balls fresh mozzarella or 3 of buffalo mozzarella, drained

6 tbsp. extra-virgin olive oil
about 24 leaves fresh basil, torn into small sections
sea salt and freshly ground black pepper

Slice tomatoes and mozzarella into even-sized slices, cubes, or chunks. Put them into a salad bowl and toss together gently. Sprinkle with olive oil and mix together again. Add basil, torn into pieces. Sprinkle with salt and pepper to taste and mix again. Let stand for about 15 minutes before serving. Alternatively, arrange the sliced tomatoes flat on a platter, cover each slice of tomato with a slice of mozzarella, and then scatter basil over slices before dressing with olive oil, sea salt, and freshly ground black pepper.

Serves 6

lebanese fatoush salad

see variations page 116

This Middle Eastern salad, especially popular in Lebanon and Syria, consists of a chilled mixed salad tossed with small cubes of toasted bread. The texture of the toasted bread adds an unusual quality.

2 or 3 fresh ripe tomatoes, cubed
1 small cucumber, peeled, quartered lengthwise, and chopped
1 medium green bell pepper, seeded, ribbed, and diced
5 scallions, chopped
1/2 small head lettuce, shredded
2 tbsp. finely chopped fresh flat-leaf parsley

1 tbsp. finely chopped fresh mint or 1 tsp. dried mint
1 pita bread (or 2–3 slices of bread), toasted and cut into cubes
for the dressing
equal amounts of olive oil and lemon juice
sea salt and freshly ground black pepper to taste

Combine the vegetables, herbs, and bread in a large bowl. Make the dressing and pour it over the salad, toss well, and chill for 30-60 minutes before serving. For an authentic Arabic flavor, the dressing should be made of equal parts of oil and lemon juice. However, you may prefer to use more oil—perhaps 2 to 3 parts of oil to 1 part lemon juice.

Serves 4

greek salad

see variations page 117

Greek salad, or *horiatiki*, is a rough country salad of juicy tomatoes, crisp cucumber, sliced red onion, green bell pepper, crumbly feta cheese, and plump Kalamata olives. Serve this delightful combination as a side dish or as a light meal with some crusty bread.

5 tbsp. extra-virgin olive oil
1 1/2 tbsp. lemon juice
1/2 tsp. dried oregano
1/4 tsp. sea salt
1/4 tsp. freshly ground black pepper, plus extra
   to serve

3 ripe tomatoes, cut into wedges
1/2 red onion, thinly sliced into rings
1/2 cucumber, peeled and sliced
1/2 green bell pepper, cubed
1/4 lb. feta cheese, crumbled
16 Kalamata olives

To make the dressing, put the olive oil, lemon juice, oregano, salt, and pepper in a small jar with a screwtop lid. Shake to combine.

Put all the salad ingredients in a large bowl. Pour the dressing over the salad and toss gently to combine just before serving. Sprinkle the salad with a little freshly ground black pepper.

Serves 4–6

lentils with lemon juice

see variations page 118

This deliciously simple lentil salad, called *adas bil hamod* in Arabic, uses the very dark, almost black, lentils that are common in Middle Eastern countries. If black lentils are hard to find, use green French lentils instead.

1 1/2 lbs. black lentils (about 3 cups)
1 quart water
2 potatoes, peeled and chopped
6 garlic cloves, crushed

1/4 cup chopped fresh cilantro
6 tbsp. olive oil
sea salt and freshly ground black pepper
1/4 cup lemon juice

Boil lentils in the water for 15 minutes. Add the potatoes and continue cooking until lentils are tender, approximately 15 minutes, stirring occasionally. In a separate pan, fry garlic and cilantro with the olive oil until slightly tender and the garlic is very lightly browned. Add the lentils and potatoes and cook for 10 minutes more on medium-low heat, stirring occasionally to prevent sticking or burning. Remove from heat, season with salt and pepper, and add lemon juice if serving immediately. If not, set aside to cool in the refrigerator and add lemon juice just before serving. Serve hot or cold with pita bread as an appetizer.

Serves 6

spinach salad with yogurt

see variations page 119

This super-easy recipe is tasty and packed with a lot of flavor. *Borani*, as it is known in the Middle East, makes a great snack or appetizer.

1/2 lb. fresh spinach, washed and drained, or
    1 (10-oz.) package frozen spinach
2 tbsp. fresh lemon juice
1/4 tsp. salt

1/4 tsp. freshly ground black pepper
1 tsp. finely chopped onions
1 cup plain yogurt

In a small saucepan, bring fresh spinach to a boil. Reduce heat to low and allow to cook for 10 minutes. (If using frozen spinach, follow package directions.) Drain spinach and allow to cool for 15 minutes. Chop into very small pieces. Place pieces in a piece of cheesecloth or heavy-duty paper towel and squeeze out excess water.

In a bowl, combine spinach, lemon juice, salt, pepper, and onions. Fold the yogurt in with other ingredients. Refrigerate and serve well chilled.

Serves 6

baked feta & walnut salad

see variations page 120

This is a rustic Greek-style salad with baked feta cheese, walnuts, mixed salad greens, and thinly sliced fresh radish and zucchini, tossed with a tangy lemon-garlic dressing.

6 tbsp. extra-virgin olive oil
1 tsp. dried oregano
1/2 tsp. freshly ground black pepper
6–7 oz. feta cheese, cubed
2/3 cup shelled walnuts, halved
1 clove garlic, crushed

3 tbsp. fresh lemon juice
pinch sea salt
6 handfuls mixed salad greens of your choice
2 radishes, thinly sliced
1 zucchini, thinly sliced

Preheat the oven to 350ºF. Mix 2 teaspoons of the olive oil with the dried oregano and black pepper in a bowl, then toss in the cubed feta cheese to coat well. Arrange the feta cubes on a cookie sheet lined with parchment paper or waxed paper. Bake for 10 minutes. Place the walnuts on a separate cookie sheet and bake for 3 minutes, then roughly chop.

Put the remaining olive oil, garlic, lemon juice, and salt in a jar with a lid and shake to combine. Put the salad greens, radish slices, and zucchini slices in a salad bowl and toss with half the dressing to coat. Scatter with the baked feta and walnuts and drizzle with the remaining dressing to serve.

Serves 4

mixed bean & sun-dried tomato salad

see variations page 121

This is a great choice for your next potluck party because you can make it ahead. It tastes even better after the flavors have had time to meld.

1 (8-oz.) jar oil-packed sun-dried tomato halves
1/2 cup chopped fresh flat-leaf parsley
1/2 cup chopped fresh basil
1 (15-oz.) can red kidney beans, rinsed and drained
1 (15-oz.) can white kidney beans, rinsed and drained
1 (15-oz.) can black beans, rinsed and drained

1 (15-oz.) can black-eyed peas, rinsed and drained
1/2 red onion, thinly sliced
1/3 cup red wine vinegar
1 tbsp. sugar
1 tsp. sea salt
1/2 tsp. Dijon-style mustard
1/4 tsp. freshly ground black pepper

Drain sun-dried tomatoes in a strainer over a bowl. Reserve the oil. Put 1/2 cup of the reserved oil in a medium bowl. Discard the remaining oil. Chop drained tomatoes; place in a separate large bowl. Add parsley, basil, all the beans, and the onion to the chopped tomatoes. Stir gently to combine. Add vinegar, sugar, salt, mustard, and pepper to the reserved oil, stirring with a whisk. Drizzle over bean mixture; toss gently to coat. Cover and chill until you are ready to serve.

Serves 10

pipirrana

see variations page 122

This really substantial salad, known as *Pipirrana*, can be made into a whole meal with a fresh green-leaf salad and some crusty bread.

6 eggs
6 small or medium potatoes, peeled and cubed
1 green bell pepper, seeded and diced
1 red bell pepper, seeded and diced
1/2 onion, chopped
1 large fresh tomato, chopped

1 (6-oz.) can tuna, drained
1/2 cup green olives with pimento or anchovy, halved
1/4 cup extra-virgin olive oil
2 tbsp. distilled white vinegar
1 tsp. salt or to taste

Place eggs in a saucepan, and cover with cold water. Bring water to a boil, then immediately remove from heat. Cover and let eggs stand in the hot water for 10–12 minutes. Remove from hot water, cool, and peel. Cut eggs into quarters, and set aside.

Meanwhile, bring a large pot of salted water to a boil. Add potatoes and cook until tender but still firm, about 15 minutes. Drain potatoes and transfer to a large bowl. Toss with eggs, bell peppers, onion, tomato, tuna, green olives, olive oil, and vinegar. Season to taste with salt. Cool, refrigerate, and serve cold.

Serves 6

escalibada

see variations page 123

This Spanish salad of grilled vegetables is served all over the Mediterranean in various different combinations.

2 red bell peppers
2 green bell peppers
2 medium-sized eggplant, thickly sliced
4 medium-sized tomatoes

for the dressing
1 tbsp. chopped fresh flat-leaf parsley
5 tbsp. extra-virgin olive oil
2 tbsp. red wine vinegar
1 clove garlic, mashed

Grill the peppers and eggplant over moderate heat on the barbecue. Pierce the skins of the eggplant to prevent skins from bursting, and grill them with the peppers for 15 minutes, turning several times. When the skins of the peppers are blistered and charred, remove from heat. Wrap in a towel and put in a paper bag. Set aside.

When the eggplant slices are tender, remove them from the grill and set aside (they will take a little longer to cook than the peppers). Score the skin of the tomatoes with a cross. Grill for 5 minutes, turning occasionally. Set aside.

When peppers are cool, remove what you can of the skin, remove the seeds, and slice. Peel tomatoes and slice. Arrange all the vegetables on a platter with the tomatoes in the center. Toss together the dressing ingredients. Drizzle the dressing over the vegetables. Serve hot or at room temperature as a side dish or as a main course with bread.

Serves 6

variations

roasted eggplant & mint salad

see base recipe page 91

roasted eggplant & sun-dried tomato salad
Prepare the basic recipe, scattering the roasted eggplant slices with
8 chopped sun-dried tomatoes (from a jar, drained), the feta, and a handful
of shredded basil leaves instead of the mint and cilantro.

roasted eggplant & parmesan salad
Prepare the basic recipe, replacing the feta with the same amount of shaved
Parmesan, and the mint and cilantro with freshly chopped flat-leaf parsley.

roasted eggplant & ricotta salad
Prepare the basic recipe, replacing the feta with 1/3 pound ricotta and the
cilantro with fresh flat-leaf parsley.

variations

neapolitan roasted pepper salad

see base recipe page 92

neapolitan roasted pepper salad with anchovies
Prepare the basic recipe, then sprinkle 6 drained and chopped anchovy fillets over the peppers with the garlic and parsley.

neapolitan roasted pepper salad with olives
Prepare the basic recipe, then sprinkle about 12 pitted and coarsely chopped green or black olives over the peppers with the garlic and parsley.

neapolitan roasted pepper salad with feta
Prepare the basic recipe, then add 3 tablespoons crumbled feta over the peppers with the garlic and parsley. Add a final dusting of dried oregano over the salad before serving.

neapolitan roasted pepper salad with red onion
Prepare the basic recipe, replacing the garlic with 1 very finely sliced red onion.

variations

salad niçoise

see base recipe page 95

quick & easy salade niçoise
Prepare the basic recipe, replacing the fresh tuna with 1 (14-oz.) can of tuna, drained and broken into chunks. Omit marinating the tuna, and just drizzle both the salad and the canned tuna with the dressing.

salade niçoise with quail eggs
Prepare the basic recipe, replacing the eggs with 12 quail eggs, lightly boiled for 2 or 3 minutes, then carefully shelled and halved.

salade niçoise with capers
Prepare the basic recipe, adding about 12 capers, rinsed and dried, to the salad with the olives.

salad niçoise with croûtons
Prepare the basic recipe, adding a handful of crisp croûtons (page 79) to the salad with the olives and basil leaves.

variations

insalata caprese

see base recipe page 96

insalata caprese with avocado
Prepare the basic recipe, adding slices of ripe avocado to make this salad into
insalata tricolore.

insalata caprese with parma ham
Prepare the basic recipe, adding some thin strips of freshly sliced Parma ham.

insalata caprese with roasted bell peppers
Prepare the basic recipe, adding roasted bell peppers preserved in olive oil—
or roast them yourself in a medium-hot oven or under the broiler. Their sweet
flavor and soft texture works really well.

insalata caprese with grilled eggplant
Prepare the basic recipe, adding a few slices of grilled eggplant to make the
salad considerably more substantial. Use grilled eggplant preserved in olive oil or
slice and grill it yourself. Before grilling, sprinkle slices with sea salt and place in
a colander to drain, covered with a weighted plate. After an hour, rinse, dry, and
brush with a little olive oil to grill.

insalata caprese with artichoke hearts
Prepare the basic recipe, adding a few chopped, well-drained, oil-marinated
artichoke hearts.

variations

lebanese fatoush salad

see base recipe page 98

toasted bread salad with peaches
Prepare the basic recipe, adding 3 cubed firm fresh peaches to the salad
before tossing.

toasted bread salad with melon
Prepare the basic recipe, adding 2 slices melon, seeded and cubed to the salad
before tossing.

toasted bread salad with potatoes
Prepare the basic recipe, adding 4 new potatoes, boiled and cubed, for a more
substantial salad.

toasted bread salad with red bell pepper
Prepare the basic recipe, replacing the green bell pepper with a very ripe red
bell pepper.

toasted bread salad with feta
Prepare the basic recipe, adding 3 or 4 tablespoons crumbled feta cheese to the
salad with the bread before adding the dressing.

variations

greek salad

see base recipe page 101

greek salad with green olives
Prepare the basic recipe, replacing the Kalamata olives with pitted green olives.

greek salad with garlic
Prepare the basic recipe, adding 1 minced clove garlic to the dressing before adding it to the salad ingredients.

greek salad with toasted pine nuts
Prepare the basic recipe, adding a handful of lightly toasted pine nuts to the salad to give it extra crunch.

greek salad with capers
Prepare the basic recipe, adding a handful of rinsed and dried capers to the salad with the olives.

variations

lentils with lemon juice

see base recipe page 102

lentils with lemon juice & tomatoes
Prepare the basic recipe, replacing the potatoes with 2 large, fresh, firm tomatoes, cut into chunks and seeded. Stir them into the lentils once they are cooled.

lentils with lemon juice & green beans
Prepare the basic recipe, adding 2 handfuls cooked and halved green beans to the salad, mixing them into the lentils and potatoes once cooled.

lentils with lemon juice & red onion
Prepare the basic recipe, adding 1 red onion, peeled and very finely chopped, to the lentils and potatoes once cooled.

lentils with lemon juice & basil
Prepare the basic recipe, replacing the cilantro with basil. Add a final sprinkling of 6 shredded fresh basil leaves at the very end with the lemon juice.

lentils with lemon juice & pine nuts
Prepare the basic recipe, adding 2 tablespoons pine nuts to the salad, stirring them through the lentils while they are still warm.

variations

spinach salad with yogurt

see base recipe page 105

spinach salad with yogurt and raisins
Prepare the basic recipe, replacing the onions with 2 tablespoons raisins, soaked in enough cold water to cover for about 20 minutes, then drained and dried.

spinach salad with yogurt and toasted almonds
Prepare the basic recipe, adding 2 tablespoons slivered almonds, lightly toasted, to the salad with the yogurt to add some nutty crunchiness.

spinach salad with yogurt and chopped apricots
Prepare the basic recipe, folding 8 fresh or dried apricots, chopped into small cubes, into the salad with the yogurt.

spinach salad with yogurt and toasted walnuts
Prepare the basic recipe, adding 2 tablespoons roughly chopped walnuts, lightly toasted, to the salad with the yogurt to add some crunch.

spinach salad with yogurt and pomegranate seeds
Prepare the basic recipe, omitting the onions and adding 2 tablespoons fresh pomegranate seeds to the salad with the lemon juice.

variations

baked feta & walnut salad

see base recipe page 106

baked feta & pine nut salad
Prepare the basic recipe, replacing the walnuts with pine nuts.

baked feta & walnut salad with red bell pepper
Prepare the basic recipe, replacing the radishes with 1 medium-sized red bell pepper, seeded and cubed.

baked feta & almond salad
Prepare the basic recipe, replacing the walnuts with slivered or chopped almonds.

baked feta & walnut salad with baby spinach
Prepare the basic recipe, replacing the mixed salad greens with baby spinach leaves.

mixed bean & sun-dried tomato salad

see base recipe page 107

mixed bean salad with olives
Prepare the basic recipe, replacing the sun-dried tomatoes with pitted green or black olives, and increasing the amount of olive oil by 2 or 3 tablespoons.

mixed bean salad with capers
Prepare the basic recipe, replacing the sun-dried tomatoes with the same quantity of drained, rinsed, and dried capers and increasing the amount of olive oil by 2 or 3 tablespoons.

mixed bean & sun-dried tomato salad with feta
Prepare the basic recipe, adding 3 ounces crumbled feta to the salad ingredients before mixing with the dressing.

mixed bean & sun-dried tomato salad with arugula
Prepare the basic recipe, mixing in a large handful of fresh arugula leaves, just before serving.

variations

pipirrana

see base recipe page 108

spanish potato salad with watercress
Prepare the basic recipe, then toss 2 handfuls of fresh watercress leaves through the salad when it is cold.

spanish potato salad with black olives
Prepare the basic recipe, replacing the green olives with pitted black olives.

spanish potato salad with capers
Prepare the basic recipe, adding a handful of plump capers, drained and rinsed, to the salad with the eggs.

spanish potato salad with pine nuts
Prepare the basic recipe, adding a handful of pine nuts to the salad with the eggs.

spanish potato salad with chicken
Prepare the basic recipe, replacing the tuna with 1 large skinless chicken breast, roasted, and shredded.

variations

escalibada

see base recipe page 111

spanish grilled vegetable salad with pesto
Prepare the basic recipe, then drizzle a little fresh pesto (page 178) over the
salad just before serving.

spanish grilled vegetable salad with feta
Prepare the basic recipe, then crumble 3 tablespoons feta cheese over the salad
just before serving.

spanish grilled vegetable salad with pine nuts
Prepare the basic recipe, then scatter a handful of lightly toasted pine nuts
over the salad just before serving.

spanish grilled vegetable salad with fennel
Prepare the basic recipe. Grill 2 fennel bulbs, sliced thickly through the base so
that they remain intact, and add them to the salad with the bell peppers and
eggplant. Increase the quantity of the dressing slightly to allow the fennel to
be dressed.

spanish grilled vegetable salad with zucchini
Prepare the basic recipe. Grill 2 medium-sized zucchini, and add them to the
salad with the bell peppers and eggplant. Increase the quantity of the dressing
slightly to allow the zucchini to be dressed.

breads

For most Mediterranean cultures, bread is as much a
part of the whole meal ritual as sitting at the table.
The bread, delicious and plentiful, is there to mop
up the juices, cleanse the palate between mouthfuls,
and help the food onto the fork.

lebanese pizza with za'atar

see variations page 137

Za'atar, a Middle Eastern spice blend, is so versatile that it can be used on meats, vegetables, rice, and breads.

1 tbsp. roasted sesame seeds	1 cup warm water
1/4 cup ground sumac	2 tsp. active dry yeast
2 tbsp. dried thyme	3 cups all-purpose flour
2 tbsp. dried marjoram	1 tsp. salt
2 tbsp. dried oregano	6 tbsp. olive oil
1 tsp. coarse salt	4 tbsp. za'atar
1 tbsp. sugar or honey	1/2 tsp. lemon juice

To make the za'atar, grind sesame seeds in food processor or with a mortar and pestle. Add the dried herbs and mix well. Store za'atar in a cool, dark place in a ziplock plastic bag or an airtight container. When stored properly, za'atar can be kept up to 6 months.

To make the dough, dissolve sugar or honey in warm water in small bowl. Sprinkle yeast over water and stir until it dissolves. Let mixture stand for 5 minutes, until a layer of foam forms. In larger bowl, combine flour and salt. Make a well in center and pour in a third of the oil and the yeast mixture. Mix flour into wet ingredients; add more water if it is too dry. On lightly floured surface, knead dough for 15 minutes, until smooth and elastic. Shape dough into ball and put in a well-oiled bowl (using about half of remaining olive oil). Cover with moist towel and let rise in warm place until double (about 1 1/2 hours). Preheat oven to 425ºF. Roll out 6 equal circles of dough. In small bowl, mix za'atar with remaining oil and the lemon juice. Pour mixture equally onto dough circles and smooth it over surface. Bake for 8–10 minutes. Eat warm.

Makes 6

pizzette

see variations page 138

Literally translating from the Italian as "mini pizzas," these are smaller than a regular pizza, although they sometimes can be up to 4 inches across. But in this case, they are only 2 inches across or smaller, to serve as a canapé.

1 oz. fresh yeast
scant 1 cup warm water
pinch sugar
3 cups white bread flour, plus extra as required
1/4 tsp. sea salt
2 tbsp. olive oil, plus extra to grease

coarse semolina, for dusting
1 1/2 cups tomato sauce or puréed canned
   tomatoes
8 oz. mozzarella, chopped finely
bunch of fresh basil leaves
extra olive oil, for drizzling

Mix yeast and water with sugar, then add about 2 tablespoons flour. Put yeast mixture in lightly floured bowl and place it somewhere warm to rise for about 30 minutes. Put rest of flour on the counter and add salt. Knead yeast mixture thoroughly, then knead it into rest of flour, adding more water as required. Add the olive oil and knead energetically for about 10 minutes. Transfer mixture to large floured bowl and return to warm place to rise again for about 1 hour or until doubled. Preheat oven to 400°F. Take little pieces of the dough (half a palm size) in your hands and flatten onto an oiled cookie sheet, sprinkled lightly with coarse semolina. When spreading out dough, dip your fingers in cold water to bring as much moisture as possible into the dough as it bakes and to help flatten it. Top each little base with a little tomato sauce, some chopped mozzarella, and a basil leaf; drizzle with a tiny amount of olive oil; and bake for about 5 minutes or until crisp around the edges. Serve warm.

Makes about 15 very small pizzas

farinata

see variations page 139

When you first make farinata (chickpea pancakes), known as *socca* in Nice, you will be more than a little alarmed at how liquid the batter seems to be. Fear not, it will pull together quite magically as it bakes into a smooth pancake. This is the poorest of foods—just finely ground chickpeas, water, oil, and salt and pepper—and yet it manages to be one of the most addictive and delicious things to eat. Try not to eat it all before serving it to your guests! Wonderful with stracchino cheese, or with salami, or just by itself.

2 cups chickpea flour
1 1/2 quarts water

sea salt and freshly ground black pepper
4 tbsp. olive oil

Put the chickpea flour in a bowl with the water and mix together thoroughly. Add the salt and pepper and half the oil. Let the farinata batter stand for about 1 hour or even overnight, the longer the better. Preheat the oven to 400°F. Use the remaining oil to grease a shallow, 12-inch-square baking pan (or a similar size), and then pour in the batter. Bake for about 30 minutes, or until crisp on the outside and still soft in the middle. You should end up with a wide sheet of farinata no more than 1 1/4 inches thick. It is best when served warm from the oven, though it is also quite good cold.

Serves 6

focaccia

see variations page 140

Created in the little town of Recco on the Ligurian Riviera, this lovely oily and salty bread is perfect when split and filled with thinly sliced Parma ham and ripe tomatoes.

2 tsp. instant dry yeast	1 tbsp. coarse salt
1 cup warm water plus 2 tbsp.	1/4 cup olive oil, plus extra for greasing
2 tbsp. sugar	and sprinkling
3 1/2–4 cups all-purpose or white bread flour	polenta or cornmeal, for dusting

Preheat oven to 375ºF. In the bowl of a standing mixer fitted with a dough hook, mix yeast with 1 cup warm water and sugar. Stir gently to dissolve. Let stand 3 minutes until foam appears. Turn mixer on low and slowly add 3 1/2 cups flour. Dissolve salt in 2 tablespoons warm water and add it to yeast mixture. Pour in olive oil. When dough starts to come together, increase speed to medium. Stop machine occasionally to scrape dough off hook. Mix until dough is smooth and elastic, about 10 minutes, adding flour as necessary. Turn dough out onto work surface and knead a few times. Shape into ball and place in well-oiled bowl, turning to coat entire ball with oil so it doesn't form a skin. Cover with plastic wrap or damp towel and let rise in a warm place until doubled, about 45 minutes. Coat a cookie sheet with a little olive oil and a sprinkling of polenta. Once dough is doubled and domed, turn it out onto work surface. Roll and stretch dough to an oblong shape about 1/2 inch thick. Lay flattened dough on cookie sheet and cover with plastic wrap. Let rest for 15 minutes. Remove plastic wrap and sprinkle top of dough with coarse salt and olive oil, making shallow dips in dough with your fingertips. Bake for about 15 minutes, or until golden brown and crisp. Remove from sheet and cool before serving.

Makes 6 small, 3 medium, or 1 large focaccia

lebanese flatbread

see variations page 141

This soft flatbread is similar to pita bread in taste, but tends to be bigger and floppier in texture. In Arabic, it is called *khoubiz*.

6 cups all-purpose flour, plus extra as needed
1 package active dry yeast
2 cups warm water

1 1/2 tsp. salt
1 tsp. sugar
2 tbsp. oil, plus extra as needed

Sift flour into a large mixing bowl and warm in a low oven. Dissolve yeast in 1/4 cup warm water, then add remaining water and stir in salt and sugar. Remove about 2 cups flour from bowl and set aside. Pour yeast mixture into center of remaining flour, then stir in some flour to make a thick liquid. Cover with cloth and leave in a warm place until frothy. Stir in rest of flour into bowl, adding 2 tablespoons oil gradually, then beat until smooth, either by hand for 10 minutes or with electric mixer using dough hook for 5 minutes.

Sprinkle some of the reserved 2 cups flour onto a counter, turn out dough, and knead for 10 minutes, using more flour as required. When dough is smooth and satiny with slightly wrinkled texture, shape into a ball. Oil bowl, put in dough smooth-side down, then turn over so top is coated with oil. Stretch plastic wrap over bowl and leave in a warm place to rise until almost doubled, about 1 to 1 1/2 hours.

Preheat oven to 500ºF. Punch down dough and turn out onto lightly floured worktop. Knead for 1–2 minutes, then divide into 8 equal pieces. Roll each piece into a ball, then into a 10-inch round, and place on lightly floured cloth. Cover with another cloth and leave for 20 minutes. Heat a large cookie sheet or flat griddle on the lowest shelf in an electric oven

(in a gas oven select section with the most heat, probably near top). Place a round of dough on a lightly floured cookie sheet with a flat edge, then flatten and shape it evenly. Shake to ensure that it will slide off easily. Rub heated cookie sheet or griddle with wad of paper towel dipped in oil, then slide the flattened dough onto it.

Bake in hot oven for 4–5 minutes, until it puffs up like balloon. If you would like it browned on top, turn quickly and leave for a minute. Remove bread and wrap in a cloth to keep it warm and soft. Bake remaining loaves.

Makes 8 loaves

pizza all'Andrea

see variations page 142

This type of pizza, which is remarkably similar to the *pissaladière* of southern France, is very popular throughout Liguria. In Sanremo, it is named sardenea, meaning pizza with sardines. The name *pizza all'Andrea* comes from the local hero, Andrea Doria (1466–1560), who was very fond of this dish.

6 cups white bread flour
1 cup warm water, plus extra as needed
3/4 oz. fresh yeast
large pinch sea salt
4 tbsp. olive oil
2 small onions, finely sliced

3/4 cup olive oil
2 1/4 lbs. ripe tomatoes, peeled and seeded
4 oz. salted anchovies, washed and boned
2 sprigs fresh basil
12 black pitted olives
2 cloves garlic, thickly sliced

Put flour onto counter, make a hole in center, and pour in enough water to just fill hole. Crumble yeast into hole and mix gently and occasionally until just fizzing, about 10–15 minutes. Add salt and oil and knead, adding more water as required to make a soft, elastic ball of dough. Knead for at least 15 minutes. Shape dough into ball, put in lightly oiled bowl, and cover loosely with plastic wrap or clean floured cloth. Let rise in warm, draft-free place for 2–3 hours. Meanwhile, fry onions gently in a little olive oil until pale golden. Add tomatoes and simmer for about 30 minutes, or until they appear glossy and sauce is thickened. Add anchovies to sauce, and simmer for 5–10 minutes. Remove from heat. Preheat oven to 475ºF. With your fingers, spread dough about 1/3 inch thick into well-oiled shallow baking pan(s). Spread tomato sauce over dough, then add basil leaves, olives, and sliced garlic. Drizzle with a little oil, then bake for about 30 minutes or until crisp and golden around edges. Serve hot or cold.

Serves 6

garlic bread

see variations page 143

This is a really easy and very delicious way to make crispy garlic bread from the south of France. It is perfect with a bowl of soup or with some cold meats.

1 head garlic
olive oil

sea salt
1 large loaf of good rustic bread

Preheat oven to 425°F. Crush the head of garlic and place it (skin and all) in the center of a large piece of aluminum foil (large enough to encase the loaf of bread). Drizzle with olive oil and season with sea salt. Place the loaf on top of the garlic, fold the foil over to create a parcel, and bake for about 5 minutes (long enough to allow the garlic flavors to permeate the bread). Serve warm.

Serves 4–6

black-olive bread

see variations page 144

You can vary the flavor of this bread with your choice of olive, so try Kalamata olives today and niçoise next week!

3 1/2 cups white bread flour
1 tbsp. active dry yeast
2 tbsp. sugar
1 tsp. sea salt

about 1/3 cup chopped black olives
3 tbsp. olive oil, plus extra for greasing
1 1/2 cups warm water
1 tbsp. polenta

In a large bowl, mix together flour, yeast, sugar, salt, olives, olive oil, and water. Turn out mixture onto a floured board. Knead until smooth and elastic, 5–10 minutes. Set aside in warm place and let rise about 45 minutes, until it doubles in size. Punch down. Knead well again, for about 5–10 minutes. Let rise for about 30 minutes, until it doubles in size. Turn out and punch down the dough on a floured board. Place a bowl lined with a well-floured towel upside down over the dough. Let rise until doubled in size.

While dough is rising for the third time, put a pan of water in the bottom of the oven. Preheat oven to 500ºF. Gently turn dough out onto a baking pan that has been lightly oiled and dusted with polenta. Bake loaf at 500ºF for 10–15 minutes. Reduce heat to 375ºF and bake for 30 more minutes, or until done.

Makes 1 loaf

pita bread

see variations page 145

Pita bread is served at just about every meal in the Middle East. It can be used for dipping, or to make delicious sandwiches in the pocket. In the Middle East, pita is made in brick ovens, where very high heat can be achieved. It is very hard to duplicate in a home kitchen, but this recipe, combined with high heat, comes close.

1 package active dry or quick-rising yeast	3 cups all-purpose flour
1/2 cup warm water	1 1/4 tsp. salt
1 tsp. granulated sugar	1 cup lukewarm water

Dissolve yeast in 1/2 cup warm water. Add sugar and stir until dissolved. Let sit for 10–15 minutes until mixture is frothy. Combine flour and salt in large bowl. Make a small depression in center and pour in yeast mixture. Slowly add 1 cup lukewarm water, and stir with wooden spoon or rubber spatula. Place dough on floured surface and knead for 10–15 minutes. When dough is no longer sticky and is smooth and elastic, put it in large, oiled bowl. Turn dough over to coat other side with oil. Allow to sit in a warm place for about 3 hours, or until it has doubled in size. Once doubled, roll out in a rope, and pinch off 10–12 small pieces. Place balls on floured surface. Let sit, covered, for 10 minutes.

Preheat oven to 500°F and move rack to very bottom of oven. Preheat cookie sheet also. With a rolling pin, roll out each ball of dough into a circle, about 5–6 inches across and 1/4 inch thick. Bake in batches for 4 minutes until the bread puffs up. Turn over and bake for 2 minutes. Remove each pita with a spatula from the cookie sheet. With spatula, gently push down puffiness. Repeat process with remaining pitas. Immediately place in storage bags to keep soft.

Makes about 10 pita breads, depending on size

lebanese pizza with za'atar

see base recipe page 125

manakeesh bil za'atar with sun-dried tomatoes
Prepare the basic recipe, then press 2 or 3 chopped sun-dried tomatoes into the surface before spreading on the za'atar and baking.

manakeesh bil za'atar with olives
Prepare the basic recipe, then scatter a handful of chopped, pitted olives over the pizza before spreading on the za'atar.

manakeesh bil za'atar with fresh tomato
Prepare the basic recipe, then scatter 6 chopped ripe tomatoes over the pizza before spreading on the za'atar.

variations

pizzette

see base recipe page 126

pizzette with mushrooms
Prepare the basic recipe, replacing the fresh basil with 2 or 3 thin slices of cooked mushrooms per base.

pizzette with olives
Prepare the basic recipe, replacing the fresh basil with half a green or black olive and a sprinkling of a little dried oregano.

pizzette with salami
Prepare the basic recipe, adding a thin slice of salami to the topping on each base.

pizzette with anchovies
Prepare the basic recipe, omitting the fresh basil and adding 1 caper, a very small piece of anchovy fillet, and a sprinkling of dried oregano to the topping ingredients.

pizzette with marinara sauce
Prepare the basic recipe, replacing the fresh basil leaf and the mozzarella with a little finely chopped garlic and a sprinkling of dried oregano on each pizza base.

variations

farinata

see base recipe page 128

farinata with stracchino
Stracchino is a sour stretch-curd cheese that is delicious spread over squares of hot, freshly baked farinata, which are then rolled up and served.

farinata with parmesan
Prepare the basic recipe, adding 2 or 3 tablespoons freshly grated Parmesan to the batter.

farinata with onions
Prepare the basic recipe, adding 1 finely chopped, lightly fried onion to the batter.

farinata with oregano
Prepare the basic recipe, adding 1 tablespoon dried oregano to the batter.

variations

focaccia

see base recipe page 129

focaccia with fennel seeds
Prepare the basic recipe, then sprinkle top of focaccia with about 1 tablespoon fennel seeds before baking.

focaccia with onions
Prepare the basic recipe, then spread top of focaccia with 2 very thinly sliced onions, olive oil, and salt and pepper before baking.

focaccia with rosemary
Prepare the basic recipe, then sprinkle 1 teaspoon finely chopped fresh rosemary over the focaccia before making dents in surface with your fingers. Spread with olive oil and a sprinkling of salt before baking.

garlic & thyme focaccia
Prepare the basic recipe, adding 1 tablespoon chopped fresh thyme to dough with the oil and water. Sprinkle 2 finely chopped garlic cloves over the surface before making dents with your fingertips, then spread with olive oil and a sprinkling of salt before baking.

sun-dried tomato focaccia
Prepare the basic recipe, adding 4 finely chopped sun-dried tomatoes to dough with the oil and water. Just before serving, sprinkle focaccia with some shredded fresh basil leaves.

lebanese flatbread

see base recipe page 130

lebanese flatbread with cumin
Prepare the basic recipe, adding 1 teaspoon ground cumin to the yeast mixture with the sugar.

lebanese flatbread with onion
Prepare the basic recipe, then sprinkle top of bread with finely chopped onion before sprinkling with a little more oil and baking as normal, onion side down first. Flip over after 2–3 minutes to bake on the other side.

lebanese flatbread with bacon
Prepare the basic recipe, then sprinkle top of bread with finely chopped bacon before sprinkling with a little more oil and baking as normal, bacon side down first. Flip over after 2–3 minutes to bake on the other side.

lebanese flatbread with garlic
Prepare the basic recipe, then cover top of bread with minced garlic, add a little oil, and bake as normal, garlic side down first. Flip over after 2–3 minutes to bake on the other side.

variations

pizza all'Andrea

see base recipe page 132

pizza all'Andrea with sardines
Prepare the basic recipe, replacing anchovies in the tomato sauce with canned sardines, leaving them in visible chunks.

pizza all'Andrea with egg
Prepare the basic recipe, replacing the garlic in the topping with 2 sliced hard-boiled eggs.

pizza all'Andrea with capers
Prepare the basic recipe, replacing the olives in the topping with a handful of washed and dried salted capers.

pizza all'Andrea with sun-dried tomatoes
Prepare the basic recipe, adding 6 coarsely chopped sun-dried tomatoes to the topping ingredients.

pizza all'Andrea with chile
Prepare the basic recipe, adding a sprinkling of chopped fresh red chile pepper to the topping ingredients.

variations

garlic bread

see base recipe page 133

garlic bread with butter
Instead of the basic recipe, peel and mince all the garlic cloves. Mix with about 5 tablespoons sweet butter. Split the loaf in half, spread with the garlic butter, and wrap in the foil to bake at 425°F for about 5 minutes.

garlic bread with smoked garlic
Prepare the basic recipe, but replace the head of garlic with a head of smoked garlic, available from online suppliers.

garlic bread with rosemary
Prepare the basic recipe, adding a few sprigs of fresh rosemary to the garlic on the aluminum foil.

variations

black-olive bread

see base recipe page 134

green-olive bread
Prepare the basic recipe, replacing black olives with green olives.

black-olive bread with oregano
Prepare the basic recipe, adding 1 tablespoon dried oregano to the dough.

black-olive bread with garlic
Prepare the basic recipe, adding 2 minced cloves of garlic to the dough.

black-olive bread with rosemary
Prepare the basic recipe, adding 2 teaspoons finely chopped fresh rosemary leaves to the dough.

black-olive bread with sun-dried tomatoes
Prepare the basic recipe, adding about 8 chopped sun-dried tomatoes to the dough.

pita bread

see base recipe page 136

pita bread with herbs
Prepare the basic recipe, adding 1 tablespoon dried mixed herbs to the dough.

pita bread with black olives
Prepare the basic recipe, adding 2 tablespoons chopped black pitted olives to the dough.

whole-wheat pita bread
Prepare the basic recipe, replacing the all-purpose flour with whole-wheat flour.

pita bread with chile peppers
Prepare the basic recipe, adding 1 or 2 finely chopped dried chile peppers to the dough.

pita bread with sun-dried tomatoes
Prepare the basic recipe, adding 5 or 6 finely chopped sun-dried tomatoes to the dough.

cheese & eggs

When planning meals in hot weather, eggs and cheese are great substitutes for meat or fish. These dishes are great for light lunches or brunches, and many of them just need some good crusty bread and a bowl of fresh salad to accompany them.

tuna-&-caper-stuffed eggs

see variations page 164

Uova ripiene al tonno e capperi is a family favorite for picnics. It is also very good for an easy lunch, especially if you arrange the stuffed eggs on a bed of dressed lettuce leaves. Italian canned tuna in olive oil has by far the best flavor, but if you are watching the calories you can use canned tuna in water. The capers and dill pickles add a note of sharp crunchiness, but leave them out if they are not to your liking.

12 eggs, hard-boiled
1 (5-oz.) can tuna in olive oil
6 tbsp. mayonnaise
4 tsp. lemon juice

about 12 capers, rinsed and chopped
5 dill pickles, chopped
sea salt and freshly ground black pepper
lettuce leaves, to garnish

Shell the hard-boiled eggs, slice in half lengthwise, and carefully remove the yolks. In a bowl, mash the yolks with a fork. Drain and flake the tuna, then mash it into the egg yolks with the mayonnaise. Mix in the lemon juice, then stir in the capers and dill pickles. Season with salt and pepper. Pile this mixture back into the halved eggs and arrange them on a large plate. Garnish with lettuce leaves and chill until required.

Serves 6

classic spanish tortilla

see variations page 165

This mixture makes one very large Spanish tortilla, which is a bit like a frittata, or a flat omelet, or you can divide the mixture in half and make two smaller tortillas.

2 lbs. potatoes, thinly sliced
sea salt
3 tbsp. olive oil

1/2 onion, chopped finely
8 extra-large eggs

Put the potato slices in a bowl and sprinkle plenty of salt over them, working it down to the bottom of the bowl. In a large skillet, heat about 1/4 inch of olive oil. When it's very hot, add the potatoes and start to fry them. Be sure to keep stirring them so they don't stick or start to brown. After about 5 minutes, add the chopped onion. Stir the contents of the skillet, then cover it. Keep checking the pan to be sure the potatoes aren't turning brown. Turn down the heat if necessary. Stir frequently. Once the potatoes break easily under the touch of the stirring spoon, they are ready. Meanwhile, break the eggs into a bowl, add a pinch of salt, and beat them until well combined. Add the potato and onion mixture to the bowl of eggs. Drain away any excess oil that's left in the skillet at this point. Mix the potato and egg mixture well while the skillet gets very hot with no extra oil in it. Pour the mixture into the skillet. Flatten it down in the pan and keep the heat at medium for a few minutes. Put a plate over the mix and turn over the tortilla gently. When you return it to the pan, press down the sides to create the classic flat shape of *tortilla de patatas*, like a thick pancake. Turn the tortilla several times. You'll find it gets heavier with each turn. It is ready when you put a knife into it and the knife comes out clean.

Serves 8

mozzarella in carozza

see variations page 166

This is a form of snack, but still quite a heavy dish, given that it is deep-fried bread and cheese. It can be served on its own or with other very light components to make up a meal. The name means that the mozzarella is in a golden carriage, like Cinderella!

8 slices white bread, crusts removed
1 1/2 tsp. anchovy paste
8 thick slices mozzarella
freshly ground black pepper

3 eggs, beaten
canola or vegetable oil, for deep-frying
tomato sauce, to serve

Lay 4 slices of bread out on a board and spread each one with anchovy paste. Cover the anchovy paste with mozzarella slices. Season with a little freshly ground pepper and cover with the other bread slices. Squash these sandwiches together very firmly. Break the eggs into a bowl, beat them thoroughly, and slide the sandwiches into the beaten eggs. Let soak for about 15 minutes.

Meanwhile, fill a wide, deep skillet with about 3 inches of oil, and heat until a small cube of bread, dropped onto the surface of the oil, sizzles instantly. Fry the sandwiches in the hot oil until crisp and golden on both sides. Remove from the hot oil with a fish slice (slotted spatula) and drain very thoroughly on paper towels. Serve piping hot, with a bowl of tomato sauce offered separately if desired.

Serves 4

croque monsieur

see variations page 167

This traditional *croque monsieur* (French grilled cheese and ham sandwich) recipe is the closest version of the original grilled cheese sandwich served in Parisian cafés in the early 1900s.

2 tbsp. Dijon mustard
8 slices sandwich bread
1/4 lbs. baked ham, thinly sliced

2 1/2 cups grated Gruyère cheese
4 tbsp. butter, softened

Preheat the broiler. Spread the mustard on 4 slices of bread. Place a few slices of ham, followed by 1/2 cup cheese, on the mustard-side of each piece of bread. Cover the cheese with the remaining bread. Spread the butter on the outside surfaces of the sandwiches. Place the sandwiches on an ungreased cookie sheet and broil for about 5 minutes, turn over, cover with the remaining cheese, and continue cooking until they are crispy and golden brown, about 5 additional minutes. (These can also be made in a skillet.)

Makes 4

neapolitan onion frittata

see variations page 168

There are countless versions of this classic dish all over Italy, using a huge variety of ingredients. Here's a favorite version from the city of Naples.

2 oz. prosciutto or pancetta, cut into strips
1 3/4 lbs. onions, thinly sliced
6 fresh mint leaves, chopped
5 tbsp. olive oil
6 large eggs, beaten
3 tbsp. grated pecorino
2 tbsp. grated Parmesan

1 small handful fresh basil leaves, finely shredded
3 canned tomatoes, drained, seeded, and cut into strips
sea salt and freshly ground black pepper
3–4 tbsp. canola or vegetable oil

Fry the prosciutto or pancetta, onions, and mint together in a little of the olive oil, stirring regularly until the onions are soft. This should take about 10 minutes. In a bowl, beat the eggs with the cheese and the basil. Fry the tomato strips in a separate pan with the remaining olive oil for 5 minutes or until softened, and season with salt and pepper. Cool, and then stir into the egg mixture. Then stir in the softened onion mixture. Heat the canola oil in a pan large enough to take all the mixture. When a small piece of bread dropped into the hot oil sizzles instantly, pour in the egg mixture. Flatten it out with a spatula and shake the pan to even out the mixture. Keep the heat under the pan quite high, but lower it if the frittata appears to be catching on the bottom or burning. Move the mixture around, lifting up the edges of the frittata as it sets, for about 6 minutes. Cover the pan with a large lid or flat plate. Turn the frittata over onto the plate, replace the pan on the stove, and slide the frittata back into the pan to cook on the other side. Cook for about another 6 minutes, and then slide it out onto a platter to serve either hot or at room temperature (but never chilled).
Serves 4

piperade

see variations page 169

This scrambled egg dish is one of those dishes that defines the cuisine of southern France, especially that of the Basque region, where it is a local specialty. In its original version, piperade relies on the wonderful tomatoes and peppers of the region.

3 tbsp. olive oil
1 onion, finely sliced
3–4 red and green bell peppers (at least 1 of each), chopped into quite large pieces
3–4 large ripe tomatoes, peeled, seeded, and chopped

2 cloves garlic, chopped
fresh chile pepper, according to taste and heat wanted
pinch fresh thyme leaves (or 1 bay leaf)
4 eggs, beaten

Heat the olive oil in a large skillet. Gently cook the onion until it is soft. Add the peppers and cook gently for 10 minutes. Then add the tomatoes, garlic, chile, and herbs, and continue to cook until everything is soft. Add the beaten eggs to the mixture and cook as with scrambled eggs. Remove from the heat when the eggs start to thicken, and serve immediately.

Serves 2 generously

beid hamine

see variations page 170

Serve these eggs as an appetizer or as a traditional garnish for meat stews, as they might be served in Egypt. This very lengthy, slow cooking produces deliciously creamy eggs. The whites acquire a soft beige color from the onion skins, and the yolks are very creamy and pale yellow. The flavor is delicate and excitingly different from eggs cooked in any other way.

4 extra-large eggs, in shells
5 skins from 4 yellow onions
2 or 3 tablespoons olive oil

Put the eggs and onion skins in a very large saucepan. Fill the pan with water, cover, and simmer very gently over the lowest heat possible for at least 6 hours, even overnight. A layer of oil poured over the surface is a good way of preventing the water from evaporating too quickly. Remove from the pan, drain, and cool before shelling and eating.

Serves 4

saganaki

see variations page 171

Saganaki dishes take their name from the pan in which they are made. A *sagani* is a
two-handled pan made in many different materials. Serve this recipe as an appetizer,
an hors d'oeuvre, or as part of a meal made up of a varied selection of mezethes.
The key to success with this dish is to get the oil really hot—just up to the smoking point
before frying.

1 lb. kefalotyri or kasseri cheese (or pecorino
    romano)
2/3 cup flour

1/2 cup olive oil
2–3 lemons, quartered

Cut the cheese into slices or wedges, 1/2 inch thick by 2 1/2 to 3 inches wide. Moisten each
slice with cold water, then dredge in the flour. In a *sagani* or a similar pan (you can use a
small paella pan, small cast-iron skillet, or even an oval gratin dish), heat the olive oil over
medium-high heat. Sear each cheese slice until golden brown on both sides, turning the
slices over after about 5 minutes. Serve hot with a last-minute squeeze of juice from 1 fresh
lemon quarter. Offer the rest of the lemons separately so each diner can add more lemon
juice to their own portion.

Serves 6

griddled halloumi with salad

see variations page 172

The salty flavor of griddled halloumi cheese is perfect against the backdrop of a lovely fresh, crisp salad with a very garlicky salad dressing that gives the whole dish real zing.

slice 8 ripe plum tomatoes
2 cloves garlic, finely sliced
1 tbsp. chopped fresh thyme
sea salt and freshly ground black pepper
sugar to taste
2 tbsp. balsamic vinegar
2 tbsp. olive oil
1 lb. halloumi cheese, cut into bite-sized cubes

4 Little Gem or any crisp lettuce, separated into
   leaves, enough for 4–6
For the vinaigrette
4 cloves garlic, unpeeled
juice of 1 lemon
1/2 cup grapeseed oil
sea salt and freshly ground black pepper

Preheat the oven to 350°F. Lay the tomato slices on a cookie sheet. Sprinkle with the garlic, thyme, salt, pepper, a touch of sugar, balsamic vinegar, and olive oil. Roast for 1 hour or until their size has reduced by half. Keep warm. Meanwhile, make the vinaigrette. Bring a small pan of water to a boil, add the unpeeled garlic cloves, and poach for 20 minutes. Drain and peel. In a blender or food processor, place the poached garlic, lemon juice, and grapeseed oil. Pulse-blend until smooth and emulsified. Add water to achieve a pouring yet coating consistency and season to taste with salt and pepper.

Heat a griddle pan over a high heat. Cook the halloumi on both sides until a good dark crust has formed on the cheese. In a serving bowl, combine the lettuce, roasted tomatoes, and freshly griddled halloumi with 8 tablespoons of the vinaigrette (storing the remainder for future use). Toss together and serve immediately.
Serves 6

huevos revueltos

see variations page 173

This is a variation of a popular tapas dish from Seville, the southern Spanish city acknowledged as the birthplace of the tapas tradition. If you want to be faithful to the original Sevillian recipe, remove the pan from the heat while the eggs are still a little runny.

14 oz. baby spinach leaves
4 tbsp. olive oil
sea salt and freshly ground black pepper
6 large eggs or 5 extra-large eggs
1 tbsp. roughly chopped fresh flat-leaf parsley
1/2 tsp. Spanish paprika

1/2 tsp. dried oregano
1 onion, finely chopped
3 garlic cloves, crushed
scant 1/2 lbs. cooked shrimp, peeled
warm crusty rolls, to serve

Wash the baby spinach leaves, then steam them in the water that's still on the leaves, for about 1 minute, or until the leaves just begin to wilt. Drain the spinach leaves well, lightly squeeze dry, then toss in a bowl with half the olive oil and sea salt and freshly ground pepper to taste. Set aside. Break the eggs into a separate bowl, then add the parsley, paprika, oregano, and sea salt and freshly ground pepper to taste. Lightly whisk together.

Heat the remaining oil in a nonstick pan. Sauté the finely chopped onion and crushed garlic until they begin to soften but not brown. Add the shrimp and mix with the onion and garlic for 1–2 minutes. Add the spinach, and continue to toss the ingredients in the pan. Pour the seasoned eggs into the pan, and stir gently over medium heat, pausing for several moments at a time to allow the mixture to begin to set. Serve immediately with warm crusty rolls.

Serves 6

variations

tuna-&-caper-stuffed eggs

see base recipe page 147

stuffed hard-boiled eggs with shrimp
Prepare the basic recipe, replacing the tuna with 6 ounces of cooked peeled shrimp and omitting the capers and dill pickles.

stuffed hard-boiled eggs with ham
Prepare the basic recipe, replacing the tuna with 5 ounces of chopped cooked ham and omitting the capers.

stuffed hard-boiled eggs with tuna
Prepare the basic recipe, but omit the capers and dill pickles.

stuffed hard-boiled eggs with poached fish
Prepare the basic recipe, replacing the tuna with 5 ounces of cooled poached white fish (such as cod), carefully checked for bones.

variations

classic spanish tortilla

see base recipe page 148

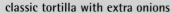

classic tortilla with extra onions
Prepare the basic recipe, adding 2 large onions, thinly sliced and fried separately until softened, to the potato and eggs before continuing as above.

classic tortilla with fresh basil
Prepare the basic recipe, adding about 20 leaves of fresh basil, torn into pieces, to the potato and egg mixture before frying.

classic tortilla with parsley
Prepare the basic recipe, adding a large bunch of freshly chopped flat-leaf parsley to the potato and egg mixture before frying.

classic tortilla with tomatoes
Prepare the basic recipe, adding 3 small tomatoes, sliced, to the potato and egg mixture before frying.

classic tortilla with cheese
Prepare the basic recipe, adding 3 tablespoons of grated strong-flavored cheese, such as Manchego, Parmesan, or strong Cheddar, to the potato and egg mixture before frying.

variations

mozzarella in carozza

see base recipe page 150

mozzarella in carozza with sun-dried tomato paste
Prepare the basic recipe, replacing the anchovy paste with the same amount of sun-dried tomato paste.

mozzarella in carozza with pesto
Prepare the basic recipe, replacing the anchovy paste with the same amount of pesto (store-bought or see page 178)

mozzarella in carozza with salami
Prepare the basic recipe, omitting the anchovy paste and adding 3 slices of salami to each sandwich. Press the salami onto the mozzarella before closing the sandwiches and soaking them in the egg.

mozzarella in carozza with parma ham
Prepare the basic recipe, omitting the anchovy paste and adding 1 slice of Parma ham to each sandwich. Press the ham onto the mozzarella and trim it to size with a pair of scissors before closing the sandwiches and soaking them in the egg.

mozzarella in carozza with olive paste
Prepare the basic recipe, replacing the anchovy paste with a thin layer of olive paste.

croque monsieur

see base recipe page 151

croque madame
This is simply a traditional croque monsieur served with a fried egg and a thin layer of hot béchamel sauce spooned over the egg.

croque provençal
Instead of the basic recipe, use sliced tomatoes, raclette cheese, and herbed mayonnaise instead of the mustard, ham, butter, and Gruyère. (You'll still need to lightly butter the outside of the sandwiches before broiling, just to prevent them sticking.)

extra-rich croque monsieur
Prepare the basic recipe, and add an extra layer of richness by spreading a bit of homemade béchamel sauce over the finished sandwich just before broiling.

variations

neapolitan onion frittata

see base recipe page 152

neapolitan zucchini frittata
Prepare the basic recipe, replacing the prosciutto or pancetta and mint with 4 cooked and thinly sliced zucchini fried with the onions. Omit the tomatoes.

neapolitan onion & bean frittata
Prepare the basic recipe, replacing the prosciutto or pancetta with a large handful of just-cooked string beans, cut into short pieces.

neapolitan onion & potato frittata
Prepare the basic recipe, replacing the prosciutto or pancetta with 2 parboiled and thinly sliced potatoes.

neapolitan onion & spinach frittata
Prepare the basic recipe, replacing the tomatoes with 2 tablespoons steamed, drained, and chopped spinach.

neapolitan leek frittata
Prepare the basic recipe, replacing the onions with the same quantity of sliced leeks.

variations

piperade

see base recipe page 155

piperade with zucchini
Prepare the basic recipe, replacing the bell peppers with sliced fresh zucchini.

piperade with mushrooms
Prepare the basic recipe, replacing the bell peppers with 5 large mushrooms, cut into chunks.

piperade with extra bell peppers
Prepare the basic recipe, omitting the tomatoes and adding 2 extra bell peppers.

piperade with onions
Prepare the basic recipe, omitting the onion, bell peppers, tomatoes, garlic, and chile, and using 3 large red onions, thinly sliced.

piperade with peas
Prepare the basic recipe, omitting the bell peppers, tomatoes, garlic, and chile. Instead, add 2 cups of fresh or frozen peas, cooked slowly, before adding the eggs.

variations

beid hamine

see base recipe page 156

dark hamine eggs
Add a teaspoon or more of ground coffee to the water to obtain a slightly
darker color all over the finished egg.

hamine eggs with carrot salad
Serve the eggs over a salad of finely grated carrots mixed with raisins,
snipped chives, and pine nuts.

hamine eggs with lettuce
Serve the eggs spooned over a bed of finely shredded, crisp lettuce leaves,
lightly dressed with olive oil, lemon juice, and salt and pepper.

variations

saganaki

see base recipe page 159

saganaki with fried egg
Prepare the basic recipe, but omit the lemon juice and lemon garnish. Top each slice of fried cheese with an egg fried in olive oil.

saganaki with fried tomatoes
Prepare the basic recipe, omitting the lemon juice and lemon garnish. In a separate pan, fry 8 thickly sliced tomatoes in olive oil, season them with salt and pepper, and lay them on top of the fried cheese just before serving.

saganaki with salad
Prepare the basic recipe. Serve the fried cheese slices on top of a salad of fresh lettuce leaves, chopped scallions, and chopped cucumber.

saganaki with mushrooms
Prepare the basic recipe. In a separate pan, fry about 20 small mushrooms in a little olive oil and a chopped garlic clove. Top the fried cheese with the mushrooms just before serving.

saganaki with garlic
Prepare the basic recipe, adding a couple of minced garlic cloves to the oil before frying the cheese to add flavor to the finished dish.

variations

griddled halloumi with salad

see base recipe page 160

griddled halloumi with bell pepper salad
Prepare the basic recipe, omitting the tomatoes (and all the ingredients used in roasting them) and the lettuce. Instead, serve the griddled halloumi on top of a salad of griddled bell peppers, cut into strips and dressed with the basic vinaigrette.

griddled halloumi with arugula salad
Prepare the basic recipe, omitting the tomatoes (and all the ingredients used in roasting them) and the lettuce. Instead, serve the griddled halloumi on top of a salad of fresh arugula, dressed with the basic vinaigrette.

griddled halloumi with mushrooms
Prepare the basic recipe, adding pan-fried mushrooms on top of the finished dish.

griddled halloumi with avocado salad
Prepare the basic recipe, adding sliced avocado to the salad.

griddled halloumi with griddled eggplant & mint
Prepare the basic recipe, adding slices of griddled eggplant. Serve the griddled halloumi on the eggplant, dressed with the basic vinaigrette and surrounded with the lettuce leaves and tomatoes.

huevos revueltos

see base recipe page 163

huevos revueltos with mushrooms
Prepare the basic recipe, adding thinly sliced pan-fried mushrooms to the eggs before cooking. Omit the spinach, shrimp, and oregano, and halve the quantity of olive oil.

huevos revueltos with onions
Prepare the basic recipe, omitting the spinach and shrimp and adding 2 more chopped onions.

huevos revueltos with bell peppers
Prepare the basic recipe, omitting the spinach and shrimp, and add 4 sliced and seeded bell peppers, lightly fried in a little oil in a separate pan.

huevos revueltos with tomatoes
Prepare the basic recipe, omitting the spinach and shrimp and using 6 large, ripe tomatoes, quartered and seeded, instead.

huevos revueltos with spinach
Prepare the basic recipe, omitting the shrimp.

pasta, couscous & rice

In Middle Eastern Mediterranean countries, rice

or couscous is usually the starch base for many

meals containing either fish or meat, although

in some cases that very Italian staple—pasta—

also appears on the menu. This chapter contains

some of the most classic and iconic

Mediterranean specialties.

spaghetti with clams

see variations page 190

As with all recipes using clams (*vongole*), please make sure they are as clean as possible before you cook them to avoid an unpleasant muddy taste or a gritty sensation under your teeth. This is a real classic from Italy.

3 1/2 lbs. fresh, live clams
6 tbsp. extra-virgin olive oil
3/4 cup dry white wine
3 cloves garlic, chopped finely

14 oz. spaghetti or vermicelli
3 tbsp. chopped fresh flat-leaf parsley
sea salt and freshly ground black pepper

Clean clams really thoroughly in several changes of fresh water to make sure you have removed all traces of sand or mud. When the water the clams are covered with is completely clear, the clams are clean. Drain clean clams and put them in a wide, fairly deep skillet with about 2 tablespoons of the oil and all the wine. Cover and heat. When the pan is very hot, shake it regularly over the heat to help the clams open up. After about 6 or 7 minutes, any clams that are going to open should have opened. Discard any closed clams. Drain the rest, reserving the liquid. Strain liquid through a fine sieve. Heat remaining oil with the garlic for a few minutes, then add clams and reserved liquid. Mix everything together and bring to a boil, then cover and remove from heat.

Meanwhile, bring a large pot of salted water to a boil. Add pasta and stir. Cover and return to a boil. Uncover and boil until tender, then drain and return to pot. Pour in clams and toss to combine. Add parsley and plenty of freshly ground black pepper, toss again, and transfer to a warmed platter or bowl. Serve at once.

Serves 4

vacation spaghetti

see variations page 191

This is the very familiar, traditional, simple raw tomato sauce for the summer, when the weather is much too hot to spend time in the kitchen. Spaghetti *sugo vacanza* is prepared by vacationing Italians all over the country.

8 large, ripe tomatoes, peeled and seeded
1 clove garlic, crushed or mashed
2 tbsp. finely chopped fresh flat-leaf parsley
9 leaves fresh basil, torn

sea salt and freshly ground black pepper
8 tbsp. extra-virgin olive oil, plus extra
   as needed
14 oz. spaghetti

Chop tomatoes roughly and put them into a bowl with the garlic, parsley, basil, salt, and pepper. Stir in the oil and let stand, covered, for at least an hour, preferably not in the refrigerator. Bring a large pot of salted water to a rolling boil, add the spaghetti, and stir, making sure all the spaghetti is immersed in the boiling water. Cover the pot and return to a boil, then remove the lid and continue to cook the spaghetti until *al dente*. Drain and return to the pot. Pour in the sauce, toss together, adding more oil if required, and transfer to a dish to serve at once.

Serves 4

linguine with pesto

see variations page 192

There are many different recipes for this very important Ligurian dressing (or uncooked sauce), as well as many ready-made versions of the sauce. To keep the pesto really green, you can add a few leaves of spinach to the basil. The amount of garlic required is largely up to personal taste, although its complete exclusion will mean this sauce is no longer a pesto but simply a basil sauce.

40 large leaves fresh basil
3 cloves garlic (more if desired)
2–3 tbsp. freshly grated Parmesan or pecorino
    cheese
2–3 tbsp. pine nuts

2–3 oz. best-quality olive oil, plus extra
    for covering
sea salt and freshly ground black pepper
1 lb. linguine
freshly grated Parmesan cheese, to serve

Ideally, this whole process of making the pesto should take place in a mortar and pestle, but if you do not have the inclination for such an intensive labor of love, a food processor will have to do. Process or pound all the basil leaves with the garlic, cheese, pine nuts, and olive oil. You should end up with a beautifully green, relatively smooth sauce with a bit of crunch. This will add depth and intensity to the pesto's color and texture. Season to taste with salt and pepper and set aside at room temperature, making sure the surface of the pesto is completely covered in a layer of olive oil to prevent oxidation.

Bring a large saucepan of salted water to a boil. Add the pasta and return to a boil. Cook until tender, then drain thoroughly. Return pasta to the hot saucepan and pour in the pesto, toss together thoroughly, then transfer to a platter. Serve with freshly grated Parmesan.

Serves 4

linguine with fish sauce

see variations page 193

For *linguine al sugo di pesce*, it is a good idea to use a fish that can withstand a fairly long cooking time without losing all its flavor and texture, you could opt for a thick swordfish steak, chopped into small cubes, and some white fish, which will flake better. In this way, there are two completely separate textures within the same dish. However, you can use any combination of fish of your choice, or even squid if you prefer. Cheese is never served with fish pasta dishes, or at least, extremely rarely.

3 tbsp. olive oil
2 cloves garlic, thinly sliced
2 or 3 tbsp. chopped fresh flat-leaf parsley
1/4 dried red chile pepper
1 swordfish steak, cubed
2 cod fillets, cubed

2 or 3 tbsp. dry white wine
1 1/4 cups puréed canned tomatoes
sea salt and freshly ground black pepper
1 lb. pasta of your choice
2 tbsp. chopped fresh mint

Pour the olive oil into a large skillet, add the garlic, parsley, and chile, and cook very gently for about 5 minutes. Discard the chile. Add all the fish and fry together for about 3 minutes before adding the wine. Stir for about 2 minutes, boiling off the alcohol, then add the tomato purée. Stir together thoroughly, season, and cover. Simmer for about 15 minutes or until the sauce is thick and glossy. Meanwhile, bring a large pot of salted water to a boil, then add the pasta. Return to a boil and cook until tender, then drain and return to the saucepan. Pour in the sauce, sprinkle with the mint, and toss everything together very thoroughly. Transfer onto a platter and serve immediately.

Serves 6

middle eastern spaghetti

see variations page 194

Koazy al-macarona is a very famous non-vegetarian dish of the Middle Eastern cuisine. This dish, with its rather odd combination of ingredients, is very easy to prepare and the results are really delicious.

4 tbsp. canola oil
2 small chickens, quartered, skin left on
1/2 cup plain yogurt
3 sticks cinnamon
1 tbsp. ground cumin
1 tbsp. ground black pepper

6 fresh tomatoes, peeled, seeded, and puréed
2 onions, chopped
sea salt
14 oz. spaghetti
3 hard-boiled eggs, shelled and sliced

Heat half the oil in a large skillet and fry chicken for about 5 minutes, turning to brown both sides. Add yogurt; half the cinnamon, cumin, and pepper; then the tomatoes. Mix together and cook the chicken, covered, for about 15 minutes. Discard cinnamon sticks. Pour the rest of the oil into another pan and add the onion, salt, and the remaining cinnamon, cumin, and pepper. Mix together and fry gently until onion is cooked. Bring a pot of salted water to a boil, break the spaghetti in half, and boil spaghetti until done. Drain the spaghetti, toss with the onion mixture, and arrange in a serving dish. Discard the cinnamon sticks. Put the cooked chicken on top and pour over the sauce. Decorate with the sliced hard-boiled eggs and serve.

Serves 4–6

tabbouleh

see variations page 195

This is a very traditional North African recipe for making a salad using bulgur (cracked wheat) as a base. You can also use large-grained couscous if bulgur is difficult to find.

1 cup bulgur wheat
4 fresh ripe tomatoes, seeded and finely
    chopped, with their juice
2 medium-sized bunches fresh flat-leaf parsley,
    finely chopped
4 scallions, finely chopped

juice of 2 lemons
3/4 tsp. sea salt
1/4 cup extra-virgin olive oil
freshly ground black pepper
2 tbsp. finely chopped fresh mint

Soak bulgur in cold water for 10 minutes. Drain in a sieve lined with damp cheesecloth, then squeeze out all the water. Transfer to a serving bowl and fluff with a fork. Stir in tomatoes with juice, parsley, and scallions. Add lemon juice, salt, and olive oil; season with pepper. Toss to coat. You can make the dish up to this point up to the day before, then just before serving, stir in mint.

Serves 4

couscous salad

see variations page 196

Couscous provides a fabulous base for all sorts of salad combinations. It is great to serve as a starter or even as a whole meal with other dishes. You will find couscous served all over the Mediterranean, including Sicily, where it is often served warm as a bed over which to serve fish stews.

1/2 lb. couscous
scant 2 cups hot vegetable stock
5 tbsp. olive oil
2 tbsp. freshly squeezed lemon juice
sea salt and freshly ground black pepper
10 sun-dried tomatoes, preserved in oil,
    quartered

2 medium avocados, peeled, pitted, and cut into
    large chunks
3 1/2 oz. black olives, such as Kalamata
good handful of nuts, such as pine nuts,
    cashews, or almonds
1/2 lb. feta, roughly crumbled
1/4 lb salad leaves such as a mesclun mix

Put the couscous into a large bowl, stir in the hot stock, cover, and let soak for 5 minutes. Make a dressing with the olive oil, lemon juice, salt, and pepper. Stir 2 tablespoons of the dressing into the couscous, and then gently mix in the tomatoes, avocados, olives, nuts, and feta. Taste, adding more salt and freshly ground black pepper if required. Toss the salad greens with the remaining dressing, divide between 4 plates, and spoon the couscous on top.

Serves 4

arabian-style rice

see variations page 197

Rice forms the basis of many meals throughout the Middle East. Often it is cooked with added ingredients, such as spices or vegetables. When cooking any Arabian-style rice, steam or bake it, tightly covered, so that it absorbs all the liquid and remains fragrant and fluffy.

2 cups long-grain rice
2 tbsp. sweet melted butter
about 4 tbsp. chopped greens (e.g., spinach or
    cabbage or tops of Brussels sprouts)

about 1 1/4 quarts cold water
1/2 tsp. salt

Wash the rice in cold water repeatedly, then cover with cold water and let soak for about 10 minutes before rinsing and draining. Melt the butter in a large skillet over medium heat, then add the rice. Add the greens and mix, being careful not to let the rice or vegetables catch on the bottom of the pan and start burning. After stirring for about 5 minutes, add the water, and season with salt. Cover tightly with a lid and a sheet of waxed paper under the lid, and let simmer until the grains have become swollen and tender and the rice has absorbed all the liquid (or about 20–30 minutes). Use 2 forks to fluff the rice before serving.

Serves 4–6

rice salad

see variations page 198

This Italian recipe (*insalata di riso*) is a great favorite for hot-weather eating, as it is light yet satisfying and includes lots of lovely fresh vegetables that make it really tasty.

1/2 lb. long-grain Italian rice
1 large carrot, cubed
2 1/2 oz. string beans (haricots verts), topped
   and tailed, and diced
1 medium potato, peeled, and cubed to same
   size as carrot cubes

1 small zucchini, topped and tailed, and cubed
2 tbsp. coarsely chopped black or green olives
1 tbsp. chopped fresh flat-leaf parsley
7 tbsp. extra-virgin olive oil
3 tsp. lemon juice
sea salt and freshly ground black pepper

Boil the rice in lightly salted water for 18 minutes, or until tender. Meanwhile, cook all the other vegetables separately, also in salted water, until tender. Drain the rice and all the vegetables thoroughly. Mix the warm, drained rice with the olives, parsley, and all the cooked vegetables. Use a very large spoon or your hands to distribute everything evenly.

Combine the olive oil and lemon juice thoroughly, then pour over the rice mixture. Mix again and season to taste with salt and pepper. Let stand for at least 1 hour, or longer, before serving. If you need to chill the salad, make sure it is at room temperature when you serve it so that the flavors come through.

Serves 4

paella

see variations page 199

This traditional Spanish dish, full of delicious fresh ingredients, involves quite a lot of cooking, so it's especially suited to celebrations. For a fantastic table presentation, small wedges of lemon can decorate the borders of the dish, and branches of aromatic herbs can be placed in the middle.

1 generous cup good-quality olive oil
6 oz. chorizo, thinly sliced
1/4 lb. pancetta, finely diced
2 cloves garlic, finely chopped
1 large Spanish onion, finely diced
1 red bell pepper, diced
1 tsp. fresh thyme leaves
1 tsp. red pepper flakes
2 cups Calasparra (Spanish short-grain) rice (or substitute bomba or Arborio)
1 tsp. paprika
1/2 cup dry white wine

4 cups chicken stock, heated with 1/4 tsp.
8 boneless chicken thighs, each chopped in half and browned
18 small clams, cleaned
1/4 lb. fresh or frozen peas
4 large fresh tomatoes, seeded and diced
1 head garlic, cloves separated and peeled
12 raw jumbo shrimp, in shells
1 lb. squid, cleaned and chopped into bite-sized pieces
5 tbsp. chopped fresh flat-leaf parsley
saffron strands

Heat half the olive oil in a paella dish or heavy-based saucepan. Add chorizo and pancetta and fry until crisp. Add garlic, onion, and red pepper, and heat until softened. Add thyme, red pepper flakes, and rice, and stir until all the grains of rice are coated and glossy. Now add paprika and wine, and when the mixture is bubbling, pour in hot chicken stock. Add chicken thighs and cook for 5–10 minutes. Now add clams to the pan. Add peas and chopped tomatoes and continue to cook gently for another 10 minutes.

Meanwhile, heat the remaining oil with the whole garlic cloves in a separate pan and add the shrimp once the garlic is softened. Fry quickly for a minute or two, then add shrimp to the paella. Repeat with the squid, frying them quickly for 2 or 3 minutes with the whole garlic cloves (you may need to add a little extra oil), and then add them to paella. Discard garlic cloves. Scatter the chopped parsley over the paella and serve immediately.

Serves 8

spaghetti with clams

see base recipe page 175

spaghetti with clams & tomato
Prepare the basic recipe, adding 3 fresh and very ripe, chopped, and seeded tomatoes to the pan with the garlic before adding the clams.

spaghetti with clams & chile pepper
Prepare the basic recipe, adding 1 or 2 dried red chile peppers, finely chopped, to the garlic before adding the clams.

spaghetti with clams & mussels
Prepare the basic recipe, substituting mussels for half of the clams. Bear in mind that the mussels might take a minute or two longer to steam open depending on their size.

variations

vacation spaghetti

see base recipe page 176

vacation spaghetti with mozzarella
Prepare the basic recipe, adding a handful of chopped mozzarella to the
spaghetti and sauce as you toss them together.

vacation spaghetti with black olives
Prepare the basic recipe, adding a handful of coarsely chopped pitted black olives
to the tomato sauce before letting it stand.

vacation spaghetti with capers
Prepare the basic recipe, replacing the basil with a heaping tablespoonful of
rinsed and dried capers, coarsely chopped.

vacation spaghetti with green bell pepper
Prepare the basic recipe, adding a seeded green bell pepper, chopped into small
cubes, to the tomato sauce before letting it stand.

vacation spaghetti with ricotta
Prepare the basic recipe, adding 3 tablespoons ricotta to the tomato sauce and
spaghetti when you toss them together.

variations

linguine with pesto

see base recipe page 178

gnocchi with pesto
Pesto is also delicious when used to dress freshly cooked potato gnocchi.

linguine with pesto & string beans
Prepare the basic recipe, adding a handful of fresh string beans to the boiling water with the pasta and cooking them together, before draining and dressing with the pesto.

linguine with pesto & walnuts
Prepare the basic recipe, adding 2 or 3 tablespoons lightly toasted walnuts to the pasta and pesto when tossing everything together before serving.

linguine with pesto & extra pine nuts
Prepare the basic recipe, adding 2 or 3 extra tablespoons lightly toasted pine nuts to the pasta and pesto when tossing everything together for a little added crunch.

linguine with pesto & tomatoes
Prepare the basic recipe, adding 3 ripe tomatoes, seeded, peeled, and chopped into small cubes, to the pasta and pesto when tossing everything together.

linguine with fish sauce

see base recipe page 179

linguine with scallop sauce
Prepare the basic recipe, replacing the swordfish and cod with 8 large scallops, cut into quarters. Simmer the scallops in the tomato sauce for just 5 minutes to prevent them from becoming rubbery.

linguine with extra spicy fish sauce
Prepare the basic recipe, increasing the amount of chile pepper by as much as 1 whole dried red chile pepper or equivalent chili powder to give the finished sauce extra fire. Be careful, however, not to add so much chile that the flavor of the fish is overwhelmed.

linguine with fish sauce & mussels
Prepare the basic recipe, adding about 12 cooked and shelled mussels to the sauce about halfway through the simmering stage.

variations

middle eastern spaghetti

see base recipe page 180

spicy middle eastern spaghetti
Prepare the basic recipe, adding 2 whole dried red chile peppers to the onion and spice mixture. Discard chiles with the cinnamon sticks.

middle eastern spaghetti with fish
Prepare the basic recipe, replacing the chicken with thick, skinless fish fillets. Reduce the cooking time by about half so that the fish does not overcook.

middle eastern spaghetti with lamb
Prepare the basic recipe, replacing the chicken with 8–12 small lamb chops or cutlets.

variations

tabbouleh

see base recipe page 182

tabbouleh with olives
Prepare the basic recipe, adding about 20 pitted and roughly chopped green olives to the salad with the tomatoes, parsley, and scallions.

spicy tabbouleh
Prepare the basic recipe, adding 1 fresh chile pepper, seeded and finely chopped, to the salad with the tomatoes, parsley, and scallions.

tabbouleh with tuna
Prepare the basic recipe, adding 1 (5-oz.) can drained, flaked tuna to the salad with the tomatoes, parsley, and scallions.

tabbouleh with chickpeas
Prepare the basic recipe, adding about 1 cup drained, cooked (or canned) chickpeas to the salad with the tomatoes, parsley, and scallions. You might like to increase the quantity of the dressing slightly as the chickpeas will soak it up.

variations

couscous salad

see base recipe page 185

couscous salad with toasted almonds
Prepare the basic recipe, replacing the mixed nuts with a good handful of lightly toasted slivered almonds.

couscous salad with apricots
Prepare the basic recipe, replacing the olives with the same quantity of dried or fresh apricots, chopped into olive-sized pieces.

couscous salad with figs
Prepare the basic recipe, replacing the olives with 6 firm fresh figs, unpeeled, (or 6 soft dried figs), cut into olive-sized pieces.

couscous salad with tuna
Prepare the basic recipe, replacing the feta with 1 (5-oz.) can tuna, drained and flaked.

couscous salad with roasted bell peppers
Prepare the basic recipe, adding 2 roasted bell peppers, skinned and seeded and cut into strips, to the couscous with the tomatoes.

variations

arabian-style rice

see base recipe page 186

arabian-style rice with spices
Prepare the basic recipe, adding 1/2 teaspoon ground cinnamon and a pinch of
ground cloves to the rice with the butter. Fry together before adding the
greens. You can omit the greens if you wish.

arabian-style rice with lentils
Prepare the basic recipe, but replace greens with 4 tablespoons cooked lentils.

arabian-style rice with fresh herbs
Prepare the basic recipe, adding freshly chopped herbs such as cilantro, mint,
and flat-leaf parsley at the very end. You can omit the greens if you wish.

arabian-style rice with chicken or duck
Prepare the basic recipe, but replace the greens with 4 or 5 tablespoons finely
shredded, cooked chicken or duck meat (or keep the greens as well).

arabian-style rice with nuts
Prepare the basic recipe, adding 4 tablespoons slivered almonds or pine nuts to
the rice with the butter. You can omit the greens if you wish.

variations

rice salad

see base recipe page 187

rice salad with pesto
Prepare the basic recipe, halving the amount of lemon juice and adding 2 or 3 tablespoons fresh pesto (page 178) to the olive oil and lemon juice dressing.

rice salad with chicken
Prepare the basic recipe, adding 2 cooked, skinless chicken breasts, cut into small cubes, to the rice with the vegetables before mixing with the dressing.

rice salad with tuna
Prepare the basic recipe, adding 1 (5-oz.) can tuna, drained and flaked, to the rice with the vegetables before mixing with the dressing.

rice salad with capers
Prepare the basic recipe, adding about 15 plump capers, rinsed and dried and roughly chopped, to the rice with the olives.

rice salad with anchovies
Prepare the basic recipe, adding 1 (2-oz.) can anchovies in oil, drained and chopped, to the rice with the olives.

variations

paella

see base recipe page 188

paella with rabbit
Prepare the basic recipe, replacing the chicken with 1 whole rabbit, jointed
(but keep the chicken stock).

paella with mussels
Prepare the basic recipe, replacing the clams with about 20 cleaned
fresh mussels.

paella with artichokes
Prepare the basic recipe, adding 8 fresh artichoke bases to the paella with the
chicken thighs.

paella with bell peppers
Prepare the basic recipe, adding 2 red bell peppers, seeded and cut into chunks,
with the peas and tomatoes.

meat & poultry

Meat dishes in the Mediterranean, particularly in Islamic countries, tend to favor beef or lamb over pork. However, many of the palate-tingling spice and herb combinations used to flavor the meat also work brilliantly with pork, so these have been included here as variations.

skewered lamb kebabs

see variations page 221

The key to tender lamb *souvlaki* is the marinade, so don't skimp on the timing (even though it takes three days!). The longer the kebabs marinate, the better this *souvlaki arnisio* will taste!

8–10 lbs. leg of lamb, trimmed and boned, cut
    in 1-inch cubes
for marinade 1
1 cup olive oil
1 tsp. ground cumin
1 tsp. dried Greek oregano
2 bay leaves, crushed
sea salt and cracked peppercorns

for marinade 2
1 cup chopped green bell peppers
2 medium onions, chopped
1/2 cup tomato paste (or 1/4 cup tomato paste
    and 1/4 cup water)
for marinade 3
1/4 cup port wine
1/4 cup red wine vinegar
1/4 cup fresh lemon juice

Mix the first marinade in a bowl, add lamb, and stir well to coat. Cover and refrigerate overnight. The following day, add the ingredients in marinade 2, stir well, cover, and refrigerate overnight. The next day, add the ingredients in marinade 3, stir well, cover, and refrigerate overnight. Soak small wooden skewers (5–8 inches long) in water for an hour or more. Thread the lamb on the skewers, leaving a little space between pieces. They can be cooked under the broiler, on the barbecue, or even in a hot skillet on the stovetop. Whichever cooking method you use, turn frequently until crispy brown on all sides (about 15 minutes). Serve hot on the skewers with other mezethes accompanied by lemon wedges and crusty bread.

Serves 12

barbecued or grilled lamb cutlets

see variations page 222

For this deliciously simple way of enjoying lamb, which in Italian is called "finger burn" (*agnello a scottadito*) because you must eat it piping hot with your fingers, you need tender little lamb cutlets and a lovely hot, even heat with which to cook them to perfection. You could follow the same recipe using small chicken drumsticks or pork spareribs.

12 small lamb cutlets
3 cloves garlic, mashed very fine
6 tbsp. extra-virgin olive oil

3 tbsp. fresh rosemary leaves, as finely chopped
   as possible
sea salt and freshly ground black pepper

Wipe and trim the cutlets, then pierce each one in 3–4 places so that the garlic and rosemary rub can really permeate the meat. Mix the garlic with the oil and rosemary, and beat until thickened and emulsified, seasoning to taste. Spread the mixture over the meat and rub it in thoroughly. Let stand for about 10 minutes, then grill quickly until seared on both sides, turning only once. You should have almost charred, blackened meat on the outside and deliciously juicy pink meat on the inside.

Serves 4

lamb tagine

see variations page 223

The beauty of this dish is that, like all spicy casseroles, it benefits from being made the day before and reheated. It even may be frozen well in advance of a party. The couscous can also be prepared in advance, and reheated in a microwave or a low oven.

1/3 lb. dried apricots, halved
2/3 cup boiling water, plus extra as needed
3 tbsp. olive oil
1 2/3 lb. raw diced leg of lamb
1 large onion, finely chopped
2 garlic cloves, thinly sliced
1 tsp. ground cumin
1 tsp. ground coriander
1 tsp. ground cinnamon
1 (14-oz.) can tomatoes
1 1/2 cups lamb or chicken stock

pinch saffron threads
sea salt
3 tbsp. almond meal
4 large zucchini, cut into large pieces
1 butternut squash, weighing approximately
    1 1/4 lbs., peeled and diced
4 tomatoes, skinned and quartered
2 tsp. harissa, plus extra as needed
2 tbsp. chopped fresh flat-leaf parsley
couscous, to serve

Place the apricots in a bowl and cover with the boiling water. Let soak for 2 hours. Preheat the oven to 350°F. Heat 2 tablespoons of the olive oil in a flameproof casserole, then brown the lamb in batches and set aside. Add the remaining oil and the onion, and cook gently for 10 minutes until soft and golden. Add the garlic and spices, and cook for 2 minutes, then return the lamb to the casserole. Add the apricots and their soaking liquid, the canned tomatoes, and lamb or chicken stock. Stir in the saffron, salt, and almond meal. Heat to simmering point, cover, and cook in the oven for 1 hour. Add the zucchini, squash, tomatoes, and harissa with a little extra water if necessary, then cook in the oven for 45 minutes more. Season to taste, adding extra harissa if desired. Stir in the parsley and serve with steamed couscous.

Serves 8

small spicy moorish kebabs

see variations page 224

Pinchitos morunos are eaten everywhere in Spain as a tapa, though nowadays they are made of pork, rather than lamb like Europe's first kebabs, which were brought by the Arabs from Africa.

2 garlic gloves, finely chopped
2 tsp. salt
1 tsp. mild curry powder or pinchito spice
    mixture
1/2 tsp. coriander seeds

1 tsp. Spanish paprika
1/4 tsp. dried thyme
freshly ground black pepper
1 lb. lean pork, cut into small cubes

Crush the garlic with the salt in a mortar (or with the flat of a knife on a board), then work in the curry powder or pinchito spice, coriander seeds, paprika, thyme, and pepper. Skewer the pork, 3–4 cubes to a small stick, and marinate them in a shallow dish with the marinade of garlic, herbs, and spices, turning so they are well coated. Let stand for at least a couple of hours in the refrigerator. Spread out the kebabs on a hot barbecue or on foil under a broiler. Cook them for about 3 minutes on each side.

Serves 6

empañadas

see variations page 225

These are little pastry envelopes that contain tasty fillings that can vary from meat to fruit. The recipe below is for the classic, rich beef filling. They are excellent served warm with a green salad and a glass of red wine.

For the dough
2 cups all-purpose flour
1/2 tsp. salt
2/3 cup shortening
6 tbsp. water

For the meat filling
1 yellow onion, roughly chopped
1 green bell pepper, roughly chopped
1 tbsp. olive oil
1 (8-oz.) can tomato paste
1/2 cup water
1 tbsp. distilled white vinegar
1 lb. lean steak, cut into 1-inch cubes

Preheat oven to 350°F. To make the dough, combine flour and salt in a medium mixing bowl. Cut in the shortening until pieces are the size of small peas. Add a small amount of water to slightly moisten. Form dough into a ball, then roll out to about 1/8 inch thick and cut it into 4-inch circles. Lightly flour both sides of circles and set aside.

To make the meat filling, sauté the onion and green bell pepper in olive oil in a medium skillet. Add tomato paste, water, and vinegar, and cook for 20 minutes. Add meat and coat thoroughly with the sauce. Place a large spoonful of meat filling in the center of a dough circle. Fold the dough into a half moon and fasten edges together by pressing the edges with a fork. Bake for about 10–15 minutes, or until golden brown.

Serves 6

potato patties with beef

see variations page 226

These potato patties with their beefy center are known as *kebba* in the Middle East. They are a deliciously tasty way to enjoy the combination of meat and potatoes in a crisp croquette.

1 lb. ground beef
1/2 cup almond meal
1/4 cup finely chopped fresh flat-leaf parsley
sea salt and freshly ground black pepper

1 lb. boiled potatoes, peeled and
    roughly mashed
2 eggs
1 1/2 cups bread crumbs
oil for frying

Put beef, almond meal, parsley, and salt and pepper in a pan over low heat. Cook for about 20 minutes, stirring occasionally. When cooked, remove from the heat and cool.

Mix the mashed potatoes with the eggs. Mash again to remove any lumps. Mix well and add salt and pepper to taste. Shape the potato mixture into tennis ball–sized rounds and stuff with the meat mixture, covering the filling with the mashed potato to enclose it completely. Slightly flatten to shape—they should look similar to a patty but no larger than your palm. Dip in bread crumbs and shallow-fry, in about 1/2 inch of hot oil, on both sides until golden brown. Serve hot.

Serves 4

circassian chicken

see variations page 227

For the best flavor, begin preparing this dish at least 2 days in advance of serving; the chicken improves with time. It keeps up to a week in the refrigerator if carefully covered. Serve warm, not hot, with a simple bulgur or rice pilaf.

2 tbsp. olive oil
6 lbs. chicken quarters, trimmed, skinned, and
    boned, then cut into smaller, even-sized
    chunks
1 tbsp. garlic, peeled and chopped with salt
2 small onions, sliced
sea salt and freshly ground black pepper
pinch saffron

1/3 cup all-purpose flour
1 tsp. white pepper, or more to taste
1 large pinch ground allspice
2 1/4 cups (1/2 lb.) shelled walnuts
1 tbsp. fresh lemon juice
3 tbsp. walnut oil
1/4 tsp. paprika

Heat oil in a 5-quart pot. Add chicken, 2 teaspoons of the chopped garlic, and the onions. Sprinkle with salt, black pepper, and saffron. Cover with water; simmer slowly and gently until chicken is tender. Drain and cool chicken, reserving the liquid. Meanwhile, toast flour in a 9- or 10-inch heavy nonstick skillet, turning it constantly until it becomes light beige. Add white pepper and allspice, and continue stirring over low heat 30 seconds longer. Remove from the heat. Lightly season with salt and black pepper. Use a slotted spoon to skim grease off the top of the chicken broth and strain. You should have 3 1/2 cups. Mix the remaining garlic with 1 cup of broth and pour over chicken to keep it moist. In a food processor, grind the walnuts and seasoned flour until smooth. Slowly add 1 cup of the chicken broth and process until smooth. Then slowly add remaining broth to make a creamy sauce. Pour sauce into the skillet, set over medium-low heat, and bring to a boil. Cook, stirring occasionally, for 20 minutes. Drain chicken pieces and place in one layer in a 9x13-inch ovenproof serving

dish. Add 1 cup of the walnut sauce and the lemon juice; mix well. Thin the remaining sauce with water to a thick pouring consistency and add salt to taste. Pour sauce over chicken. Let cool completely, cover with plastic wrap, and refrigerate for at least 2 days before serving. Gently reheat chicken in a 350°F oven until warm. Heat walnut oil in a very small saucepan, add paprika, and swirl to combine; heat just to a sizzle. Remove from heat and allow the paprika to settle. Drizzle the red-tinted oil over the dish, making decorative swirls, and serve.

Serves 12–14

chicken with peppers

see variations page 228

The sweet taste of the peppers is perfect with the chicken in this simple dish called *pollo ai peperoni*. All it needs to finish it off are some boiled or steamed potatoes and a simple green vegetable such as haricots verts.

1 large chicken, or 2 smaller chickens
4 tbsp. olive oil
3 cloves garlic, sliced thinly
1 cup dry white wine, plus extra as needed
4 juicy, thick red and yellow bell peppers,
    seeded and sliced into strips

1 lb. fresh ripe tomatoes, peeled, seeded, and
    coarsely chopped (or substitute 1 14-oz. can
    chopped tomatoes)
sea salt and freshly ground black pepper
chopped fresh flat-leaf parsley, to garnish

Clean and trim the chicken, then cut into pieces. Heat the oil with the garlic in a wide, deep saucepan for about 5 minutes, then add the chicken joints. Brown the chicken all over, sprinkling with the wine. Remove the chicken and set to one side. Add the bell peppers and tomatoes to the pan and cook together, stirring, for about 5 minutes. Season with salt and pepper and add the chicken. Stir again and cover. Simmer until cooked through, basting occasionally with white wine or water, for about 40 minutes. Serve hot or cold, but not chilled, sprinkled with parsley.

Serves 6

moroccan chicken

see variations page 229

Preserved lemon is traditionally called for in this dish, although you can use thinly sliced fresh lemon if you prefer or if preserved lemons prove hard to find.

2 tsp. paprika
1 tsp. ground cumin
1 tsp. ground ginger
1 tsp. powdered turmeric
1/2 tsp. ground cinnamon
1/4 tsp. freshly ground black pepper
1 (3–4 lb.) chicken, cut into 8 pieces (or
   3–4 lbs. of chicken thighs and legs)
2 tbsp. olive oil
sea salt

3 cloves garlic, minced
1 onion, chopped
peel from 1 preserved lemon, rinsed in cold
   water, pulp discarded, peel cut into thin
   strips
1 cup green olives, pitted
1/2 cup raisins
1/2 cup water
1/4 cup chopped fresh flat-leaf parsley
1/4 cup chopped fresh cilantro

Combine spices and pepper in a large bowl. Put chicken pieces in the bowl, coating well with spice mixture. Let the chicken stand for 1 hour in the spices. In a large, heavy-bottomed skillet, heat the olive oil on medium-high heat. Add chicken pieces, sprinkle lightly with salt (go easy on salt; the olives and lemons are salty), and brown, skin-side down, for 5 minutes. (If you are using a clay tagine, skip the browning step; heat only to medium heat and use a heat diffuser on the heating element to prevent the tagine from cracking.) Lower heat to medium-low, add garlic and onion, cover, and cook for 15 minutes. Turn chicken pieces over. Add lemon slices, olives, raisins, and 1/2 cup water. Bring to a simmer on medium heat, then turn heat to low, cover, and cook for 30 minutes, until the chicken is cooked through and quite tender. Mix in fresh parsley and cilantro just before serving. Adjust seasoning to taste. Serve with couscous, rice, or rice pilaf.
Serves 4–6

lebanese kofta meatballs

see variations page 230

The original name of this Middle Eastern specialty is *dawood basha*. In many parts of the Middle East, the mixture for kofta meatballs is sold already seasoned. To make it, mix 1 pound lean ground beef with 1/2 onion and 1/2 bunch of fresh parsley leaves in a food processor; add salt and pepper to taste. Pomegranate syrup (or pomegranate molasses) is sold in all good Middle Eastern stores.

1 lb. kofta meat
1 tbsp. vegetable oil
1 large onion, finely chopped
2 garlic cloves, crushed
1 (14.5-oz.) can chopped tomatoes
2 tbsp. pomegranate syrup

1 cup water
1/4 tsp. powdered allspice
1 tsp. sea salt
1 pinch dried mint
1 pinch dried oregano

Preheat oven to 400°F. Divide kofta meat into 20 small balls. Put on a nonstick rimmed cookie sheet and bake for 30 minutes. Flip meatballs every 10 minutes for even cooking. Remove and set aside. In a large pot, heat oil, add onion, and fry until lightly browned. Add garlic and fry gently for 2 more minutes. Add tomatoes, pomegranate syrup, and water, and stir together. Gently cook for 10 minutes, then carefully add the meatballs and remaining ingredients. Bring to a boil. Cover and cook over low heat for 20 more minutes or until mixture thickens. Serve hot with cooked rice.

Serves 4–6

chicken roasted with apricots

see variations page 231

This classic Middle Eastern dish is known as *djedjad* in Arabic. It is a wonderfully aromatic way to cook chicken, delicately scented, and very elegant.

1/4 cup sweet butter
1/4 cup honey
1 tbsp. rose water
1 tsp. sea salt
1/2 tsp. freshly ground black pepper

1 (4-lb.) whole chicken, cleaned
1 lb. ripe fresh apricots, pitted and halved
1 tbsp. sugar
1/2 cup toasted slivered almonds, to garnish

Preheat oven to 425°F. Mix together the butter, honey, rose water, salt, and pepper. Rub this mixture all over the chicken, both inside and out. Place the chicken in a roasting pan and slide into the oven. Turn the chicken over several times as it roasts to brown all sides thoroughly. When the chicken is cooked through, lower the oven temperature to 350°F. Remove the chicken, joint it, and set it aside to keep warm. Add the apricots and the sugar to the pan juices, then stir to combine. Return the chicken pieces to the roasting pan. Baste chicken joints and apricots with the pan juices and continue roasting for 20 minutes. Transfer to a warm platter, pour the juices on top, and sprinkle with the almonds to serve.

Serves 6–8

variations

skewered lamb kebabs

see base recipe page 201

skewered pork kebabs
Prepare the basic recipe, replacing the lamb with cubes of pork.

skewered chicken kebabs
Prepare the basic recipe, replacing the lamb with cubes of chicken.

skewered beef kebabs
Prepare the basic recipe, replacing the lamb with cubes of beef.

mixed meat kebabs
Prepare the basic recipe, using a combination of different meats cooked together, making sure they are all cut to the same size so that they can cook evenly.

variations

barbecued or grilled lamb cutlets

see base recipe page 202

barbecued or grilled lamb cutlets with lemon
Prepare the basic recipe, adding the grated zest of 1/2 lemon and the juice
of the other 1/2 lemon to the garlic and rosemary rub to give the cutlets a
zesty flavor.

barbecued or grilled pork sparerib chops
Prepare the basic recipe, replacing the lamb with small pork sparerib chops.

barbecued or grilled chicken drumsticks
Prepare the basic recipe, replacing the lamb with 12 skinless chicken
drumsticks.

barbecued or grilled lamb cutlets with oregano
Prepare the basic recipe, replacing the rosemary with finely chopped
fresh oregano.

variations

lamb tagine

see base recipe page 205

vegetable tagine
Prepare the basic recipe, but omit the lamb. Increase the quantities of
vegetables by about half again and add 2 (15-oz.) cans of chickpeas, drained.

chicken tagine
Prepare the basic recipe, replacing the lamb with the same amount of
chicken (dark meat from drumsticks and thighs if possible).

pigeon tagine
Prepare the basic recipe, replacing the lamb with the same amount of
pigeon breasts, skin removed.

beef tagine
Prepare the basic recipe, using cubed lean stewing beef instead of the lamb,
and follow the basic recipe, slightly increasing the cooking time as necessary
to allow the beef to become tender all the way through.

small spicy moorish kebabs

see base recipe page 206

small spicy moorish beef kebabs
Prepare the basic recipe, replacing the pork with cubes of tender beef steak.

small spicy moorish chicken kebabs
Prepare the basic recipe, replacing the pork with cubes of tender, skinless chicken breast.

small spicy moorish turkey kebabs
Prepare the basic recipe, replacing the pork with cubes of tender, skinless turkey breast.

small spicy moorish lamb kebabs
Prepare the basic recipe, replacing the pork with cubes of tender boneless lamb.

empañadas

see base recipe page 209

pork empañadas
Prepare the basic recipe, replacing the beef with pork and proceeding with
the basic recipe.

apple empañadas
Prepare the basic pastry, then make a sweet apple filling. In a small pan,
combine 2 1/2 cups peeled, cored, and sliced apples; 1 cup sugar; 1 teaspoon
ground cinnamon; and 1/2 teaspoon ground nutmeg. Cook gently over low
heat until the apples are softened. Let cool, then fill the pastry circles as in
the basic recipe.

lamb empañadas
Prepare the basic recipe, replacing the beef with lamb.

turkey empañadas
Prepare the basic recipe, replacing the beef with turkey.

chicken empañadas
Prepare the basic recipe, replacing the beef with chicken.

variations

potato patties with beef

see base recipe page 210

potato patties with pork & pine nuts
Prepare the basic recipe, replacing the ground beef with ground pork and the almond meal with chopped pine nuts.

potato patties with kofta beef
Prepare the basic recipe, but replace the plain ground beef with kofta beef (see recipe, page 219).

potato patties with ground lamb
Prepare the basic recipe, replacing the ground beef with ground lamb, and adding a little finely chopped fresh mint to the meat mixture.

variations

circassian chicken

see base recipe page 212

circassian turkey
Prepare the basic recipe, replacing the chicken with 1/4 of a small turkey, which will need to be stewed to make necessary broth.

circassian duck
Prepare the basic recipe, replacing the chicken with duck. The result will be a great deal richer, and still delicious. You will need to make the broth using the duck; degrease with care as it will be a lot fattier.

circassian veal
Prepare the basic recipe, replacing the chicken with boneless veal chunks, which will need to be stewed to create a veal broth as in the original recipe.

circassian chicken with almonds
To give the dish a nutty flavor, substitute the walnuts for blanched almonds, and use sweet almond oil in place of the walnut oil.

variations

chicken with peppers

see base recipe page 215

rabbit with peppers
Prepare the basic recipe, replacing the chicken with a joint of rabbit (enough to feed 6). Before using, soak the rabbit overnight in water with a splash of vinegar before draining and drying.

chicken with peppers & eggplant
Prepare the basic recipe, replacing 1 bell pepper with 1 eggplant, previously cut into large cubes, salted and allowed to drain for 1 hour, rinsed, and dried before using.

spicy chicken with peppers
Prepare the basic recipe, giving a little heat to the dish with 1 or 2 fresh chile peppers, chopped, added with the peppers and tomatoes.

chicken with peppers & red wine
Prepare the basic recipe, replacing the white wine with dry red wine.

variations

moroccan chicken

see base recipe page 216

moroccan pork with lemon, olives & capers
Prepare the basic recipe, replacing the chicken with large chunks of lean pork and adding 1 tablespoon capers, rinsed, to the dish with the olives and lemon.

moroccan lamb with lemon & olives
Prepare the basic recipe, replacing the chicken with large chunks of boneless lamb.

moroccan rabbit with lemon & olives
Prepare the basic recipe, replacing the chicken with jointed rabbit. Before using, soak the rabbit overnight in a bowl of water with a splash of vinegar. Drain and dry the rabbit joints, before proceeding with the recipe.

moroccan pheasant with lemon & olives
Prepare the basic recipe, replacing the chicken with 2 or 3 jointed young pheasants.

moroccan guinea fowl with lemon & olives
Prepare the basic recipe, replacing the chicken with jointed guinea fowl.

variations

lebanese kofta meatballs

see base recipe page 219

lebanese kofta lamb meatballs
Prepare the basic recipe, replacing the ground beef in the kofta meat with ground lamb.

lebanese kofta chicken meatballs
Prepare the basic recipe, replacing the ground beef in the kofta meat with ground chicken.

lebanese kofta pork meatballs
Prepare the basic recipe, replacing the ground beef in the kofta meat with ground pork.

extra spicy lebanese kofta meatballs
Prepare the basic recipe, adding half a teaspoon ground chili powder to the recipe instead of the allspice.

variations

chicken roasted with apricots

see base recipe page 220

chicken roasted with peaches
Prepare the basic recipe, replacing the apricots with the same quantity of ripe fresh peaches.

chicken roasted with plums
Prepare the basic recipe, replacing the apricots with the same quantity of ripe fresh plums.

chicken roasted with nectarines
Prepare the basic recipe, replacing the apricots with the same quantity of ripe fresh nectarines.

guinea fowl roasted with apricots
Prepare the basic recipe, replacing the chicken with a large guinea fowl. Bear in mind that they tend to be smaller than chickens, so reduce all the quantities slightly so as not to overpower the flavor of the bird's meat.

chicken roasted with dried apricots
If fresh apricots are unavailable, you can use dried apricots, soaked for an hour or so in warm water to just cover, then drained. Add a little water or chicken stock to make up for the loss of juice.

fish & seafood

Fresh fish and seafood is a central part of the
Mediterranean diet. Really fresh fish and seafood
will never smell fishy, but will have the scent of the
salty sea—when shopping for fish or seafood, you
should always trust your nose.

seafood brochettes

see variations page 247

Cooking fish or seafood on skewers can be done on the barbecue, in the oven, or under the broiler. These brochettes look very pretty and taste wonderful.

1/2 lb. cod fillets, halved
1/2 lb. scallops (halved, if large)
1 lb. large shrimp, shelled and deveined
2 green or red bell peppers, seeded and cut into chunks
1 bunch large scallions, cut into chunks, or 2 red onions, cut into segments
For the marinade
5 tbsp. fresh lemon juice

1/4 cup dry white wine
1/2 cup very finely chopped fresh flat-leaf parsley
1/2 cup extra-virgin olive oil
3 cloves garlic, very finely chopped
1 small ripe tomato, very finely chopped
1 tbsp. mild chili powder
3/4 tsp. sea salt
3/4 tsp. dried oregano

Soak 8 or 10 small wooden skewers (5–8 inches long) in water for an hour or more. Thread an alternating combination of cod, scallops, shrimp, bell peppers, and scallions or onion pieces on each of the skewers. Place brochettes in a large, shallow dish or baking pan. Make the marinade by mixing the ingredients in a jar with a tight-fitting lid. Shake well and pour over the brochettes. Marinate in the refrigerator at least 4 hours, turning occasionally. Preheat broiler. Remove brochettes from pan, reserving marinade. Broil brochettes 5 inches from heat for 5–7 minutes on each side, or until seafood is opaque and firm to the touch. Do not overcook. Place brochettes on a warmed serving platter. Bring reserved marinade to a boil and pour over brochettes to serve.

Serves 4–6

serrano ham & shrimp tostadas

see variations page 248

The Spanish *tostada* is probably one of Spain's most famous midmorning snacks. It is very similar to the many kinds of snacks found around the Mediterranean, where a bread base is used to hold a variety of delicious ingredients.

4 slices crusty bread
1 (14-oz.) jar tomato sauce or the same amount
   of homemade tomato sauce
3 paper-thin slices Serrano ham, cut into strips

8 jumbo shrimp (peeled and deveined,
   tails left on)
4 heaping tbsp. grated Manchego cheese
10 fresh basil leaves

Preheat the broiler. Place bread slices on counter and spread a generous amount of tomato sauce over each piece. Place the Serrano ham strips on top of the sauce. Place 2 shrimp on top of the Serrano ham. Sprinkle the Manchego cheese over the top, and then add the basil. Slide under the broiler and cook until done, then transfer onto plates and serve at once.

Serves 4

fresh tuna & cherry tomato kebabs

see variations page 249

This is a delicious way to enjoy succulent chunks of fresh tuna and an ideal recipe to make on the barbecue. Just don't skimp on the marinating time, or the fish will turn out dry.

14 oz. fresh tuna, cut into cubes about the
    same size as the cherry tomatoes
20 cherry tomatoes
For the marinade
4 tbsp. extra-virgin olive oil
2 tbsp. fresh lemon juice

2 tbsp. finely chopped fresh flat-leaf parsley
2 cloves garlic, minced or crushed
1 tsp. sea salt
1/2 tsp. freshly ground black pepper
lemon wedges, for serving

Thread the tuna and cherry tomatoes alternately onto each skewer, using about 6 to 8 skewers, depending how many cubes of tuna you have cut. Lay the skewers in a shallow pan. Mix together the marinade ingredients in a small bowl until well combined, then pour over the tuna and tomato skewers. Marinate, covered, in the refrigerator for 1 hour or longer, turning the skewers halfway through.

Cook the skewers under a hot broiler for 8 minutes, turning and brushing regularly with the marinade. Serve the skewers with lemon wedges for squeezing.

Serves 4-6

sicilian stuffed swordfish rolls

see variations page 250

In Sicily, where this dish is known as *involtini di pesce spada*, this is a really wonderful way to enjoy this very typical local fish. These swordfish rolls are equally delicious served at room temperature or piping hot.

2 1/2 lbs. swordfish steak
1 large red onion
12–15 bay leaves
2 tbsp. olive oil
1 cup dried bread crumbs

For the filling
4 tbsp. pitted green olives
3 tbsp. capers
2 tbsp. chopped fresh flat-leaf parsley
6 tbsp. dried bread crumbs
4 tbsp. grated Parmesan or pecorino cheese
5 tbsp. olive oil

Bone and skin the swordfish steak (or ask your fishmonger to do it for you), cut it into quarters, and slice each quarter across into 6 very thin slices. What you are aiming for is 24 slices roughly 3 by 4 inches and less than 1/8 inch thick. (But given the price of swordfish, it is wise to tolerate considerable irregularity rather than to trim lavishly—it won't show in the end anyway.) Peel the onion, cut it into quarters or sixths, depending on its size, and then separate these wedges so that you have slices of onion that are wide enough to thread on a skewer.

To make filling, chop olives, capers, and parsley together until quite fine. Stir in bread crumbs and cheese, moisten with oil, and blend thoroughly. Place a teaspoon of filling on one end of each slice of fish, roll up as neatly as possible, and spear it on a skewer onto which you have already threaded a piece of onion. Follow with a bay leaf, then another roll of fish, then a

slice of onion, and so on until you have 6 skewers, each with 4 rolls of fish interspersed with onion slices and bay leaves. Run a second skewer through each roll, parallel to the first and about an inch distant, so that the fish rolls don't spin about and break as you turn them over while they cook. Preheat broiler. When all 6 servings are ready, moisten them with oil and then dip them in the bread crumbs (they should be just lightly coated). Broil them gently for about 8–10 minutes. They can also be baked, which might be simpler if the shapes of the rolls are very irregular.

Serves 6

grilled shrimp with citrus aïoli

see variations page 251

This is a perfect way to whet appetites before the main part of the meal begins, or you can make it into a light meal by serving it with crusty French bread and a green salad.

12 oz. raw jumbo shrimp, peeled and deveined
2 tsp. extra-virgin olive oil
1/4 tsp. ground cumin
pinch cayenne pepper
pinch sea salt
pinch freshly ground black pepper

For the citrus aïoli
1/3 cup mayonnaise
1/2 tsp. grated lemon zest
1/2 tsp. grated lime zest
1/2 tsp. grated orange zest
1 small clove garlic, minced
pinch freshly ground black pepper

Preheat broiler to medium-high heat. In a bowl, combine shrimp, oil, cumin, cayenne pepper, salt, and black pepper. Toss until shrimp are well coated in seasonings. Place shrimp under broiler and cook, turning once, until shrimp are pink and opaque, about 4 minutes. Transfer shrimp to plate and refrigerate until cold.

To make the citrus aïoli, in a small bowl, whisk together all the ingredients. If you wish, you can make the aïoli ahead and refrigerate it in an airtight container for up to 2 days. Serve the shrimp on a platter, with the sauce offered separately in a small bowl.

Serves 4

steamed mussels with pesto

see variations page 252

This is a great way to serve mussels. Make sure there is plenty of good crusty bread with which to soak up all the lovely juices left in the bowl once the mussels have been eaten, and offer your guests finger bowls and plenty of napkins because this can get decadently messy!

For the pesto
2 cups fresh basil leaves (from a 2-oz. bunch)
1/4 cup coarsely chopped walnuts
5 garlic cloves (1 whole, 4 thinly sliced)
1/4 cup freshly grated Parmesan cheese
1 1/4 cups extra-virgin olive oil

1 cup halved cherry or grape tomatoes
sea salt and freshly ground black pepper
3 large shallots, thinly sliced
1 cup dry white wine
5 lbs. mussels, scrubbed and debearded
crusty bread, for serving

To make the pesto, combine the basil, walnuts, and whole garlic cloves in a food processor and pulse until fine. Add the Parmesan and roughly one-third of the olive oil, and process until smooth. Transfer the pesto to a medium bowl and add another 2 tablespoons of the oil with the tomatoes and season with salt and pepper. Use a final drizzling of the oil to cover the surface and set aside. In a very large, deep skillet or large soup pot, heat the remaining olive oil until simmering. Add the shallots and 4 sliced garlic cloves. Cook over high heat, stirring, until lightly golden, about 4 minutes. Add the white wine and a generous pinch each of salt and pepper, then bring to a boil. Add the mussels and stir for 1 minute. Cover and cook, stirring occasionally, until all of the mussels have opened, about 6–8 minutes. Discard any mussels that do not open. Add the pesto-tomato mixture and stir until the mussels are evenly coated. Transfer the mussels and broth to bowls and serve with crusty bread.

Serves 6–8

baked stuffed baby squid on a bed of fennel

see variations page 253

Sweet and tender baby squid come into their own when paired with spicy chorizo and salty feta. Served on a fragrant bed of cooked fennel, they are really wonderful.

1/2 lb. uncooked chorizo
generous 1/2 cup dry white wine
scant 1/2 lb. feta or other hard white goat's cheese
20 baby squid, cleaned, tubes and tentacles only

vegetable oil, for greasing and frying
2 fennel bulbs, thinly sliced
1 tbsp. good quality extra-virgin olive oil, plus extra to serve
sea salt and freshly ground black pepper

Put the chorizo in a saucepan with the white wine (the wine should cover the chorizo). Bring to a boil, then lower heat and simmer for 15 minutes. Remove from heat and let the chorizo cool in the pan. When cool, peel off chorizo skins and chop meat into small cubes. Put in a bowl. Chop the feta into similar-sized cubes as the chorizo, and mix with the chorizo. Carefully spoon the mixture into the squid tubes, filling tubes to three-quarters full. Fasten the opening closed with a toothpick.

Lightly oil a baking dish large enough to take all the filled squid. Preheat oven to 375°F. Heat a good half inch of vegetable oil in a very large skillet over high heat. When very hot, add the squid bodies and cook in batches, searing them for 1 minute on each side. As each batch of squid is seared, transfer to the prepared baking dish after draining on paper towels. When all the squid are seared, place the dish in the oven to finish cooking for 3–4 minutes.

Add the squid tentacles to the skillet and fry for 1–2 minutes, or until just cooked through, then drain on paper towels.

Bring a pan of salted water to a boil. Add the fennel and boil for 1 minute. Drain the fennel and place in a bowl. Drizzle with 1 tablespoon olive oil and season, to taste, with salt and pepper. To serve, place equal portions of the fennel into the center of each plate. Top each with 5 stuffed squid tubes and a few tentacles. Drizzle with a little olive oil and serve.
Serves 4

sea bass in salt crust

see variations page 254

This dramatic dish is a very special way to serve fresh fish. The crust is very thick, and it must be cracked open like a shell to reveal the perfectly cooked white fish within. It is important to protect the fish from becoming too salty—the skin of the fish will protect it all over, but use foil or waxed or parchment paper along the belly slit to prevent the salt from seeping inside the fish.

1 fresh sea bass (approximately 3 1/3 lbs.)   about 3 1/3 lbs. sea salt
2 egg whites, beaten until foaming and
    thickened

Preheat the oven to 400ºF. Clean and gut the fish carefully. Wash thoroughly and pat dry. Protect the slit in the fish's belly with a sheet of foil or waxed paper tucked inside the fish. Mix the egg whites and salt together thoroughly to make a wet cementlike texture. Find a large ovenproof dish that is larger than the fish itself to allow space for the salt crust. Line the bottom with about half the salt mixture. Lay the fish on top, then cover completely with more of the mixture. Bake in the oven until the surface of the salt crust is dark brown. This should take about 45 minutes. Take the dish out of the oven and crack the salt crust. Carefully remove the fish and brush off any excess salt before serving.

Serves 6

crisp shrimp fritters

see variations page 255

Known as *tortillitas de camarones* in Spain, these delicious fritters are wonderful served as an appetizer with a glass or two of dry white wine or chilled dry sherry.

1/2 lb. small shrimp, peeled
1 1/2 cups chickpea flour or all-purpose flour
1 tbsp. chopped fresh flat-leaf parsley
3 scallions, finely chopped

1/2 tsp. sweet cayenne or paprika
sea salt
olive oil, for deep-frying

Cover the shrimp with water and bring to a boil over high heat. As soon as water starts to boil, quickly lift out shrimp with a slotted spoon and set aside. Scoop out 1 cup cooking water and let cool. Discard remaining water. When the shrimp are cool, cover and refrigerate. To make batter, combine flour, parsley, scallions, and paprika in a bowl. Add pinch of salt and the cooled cooking water, and mix well. Cover and refrigerate for 1 hour. Mince shrimp very fine, and add to chilled batter; mix well again.

Pour olive oil into heavy sauté pan to about 1 inch deep, then heat until almost smoking. Add 1 tablespoon batter to the oil for each fritter and, using the back of a spoon, flatten into a 3 1/2-inch round. Do not crowd pan. Fry, turning once, for about 1 minute on each side, or until the fritters are golden and very crisp. Using a slotted spoon, lift out the fritters, holding them briefly over pan to allow excess oil to drain, and transfer to ovenproof platter lined with paper towels. Keep warm in low oven while frying the rest of the fritters, always making sure oil is very hot before adding the mixture. When all the fritters are cooked, arrange on a platter and serve immediately.

Serves 6

variations

seafood brochettes

see base recipe page 233

shrimp brochettes
Prepare the basic recipe, replacing all the seafood with 2 pounds of shelled
and deveined large shrimp.

baby squid & shrimp brochettes
Prepare the basic recipe, replacing the cod and scallops with 1 pound
cleaned baby squid.

scallop & mushroom brochettes
Prepare the basic recipe, using 1 pound cleaned whole scallops (medium-
sized) and 1 pound firm mushrooms of a similar size (omitting the cod,
shrimp, and bell peppers).

spicy seafood brochettes
Prepare the basic recipe, adding 1 or 2 finely chopped fresh chile peppers to
the other marinade ingredients to give the brochettes extra fire.

variations

serrano ham & shrimp tostadas

see base recipe page 234

serrano ham & shrimp tostadas with mozzarella
Prepare the basic recipe, replacing the Manchego cheese with 5 ounces mozzarella, finely chopped.

serrano ham & shrimp tostadas with tomatoes
Prepare the basic recipe, replacing the tomato sauce with 8 cubed and seeded tomatoes, divided evenly between the 4 slices of bread.

serrano ham & shrimp tostadas with avocado
Prepare the basic recipe, then scatter 2 peeled and cubed avocados over the top just before serving.

serrano ham & scallop tostadas with mozzarella
Replace the shrimp with 8 large scallops, cleaned and halved.

variations

fresh tuna & cherry tomato kebabs

see base recipe page 237

fresh swordfish & cherry tomato kebabs
Prepare the basic recipe, replacing the tuna cubes with cubed swordfish.

fresh shark & cherry tomato kebabs
Prepare the basic recipe, replacing the tuna cubes with cubed fresh shark.

spicy fresh tuna & cherry tomato kebabs
Prepare the basic recipe, adding 2 fresh chile peppers, seeded and finely chopped, to the marinade to give the kebabs extra fire.

fresh tuna & cherry tomato kebabs with cilantro marinade
Prepare the basic recipe, replacing the parsley in the marinade with chopped fresh cilantro.

fresh tuna, mushroom & cherry tomato kebabs
Prepare the basic recipe, replacing half the cherry tomatoes with small button mushrooms. Alternate fish, cherry tomatoes, and mushrooms on the skewers.

variations

sicilian stuffed swordfish rolls

see base recipe page 238

sicilian stuffed swordfish rolls with raisin filling
Instead of the basic filling, combine 4 tablespoons raisins, 5 tablespoons bread crumbs, 3 tablespoons pine nuts, and 2 tablespoons chopped parsley. Moisten with water and season with salt and pepper, then proceed with the basic recipe.

spicy sicilian stuffed swordfish rolls
Prepare the basic recipe, adding 2 seeded and finely chopped fresh chile peppers to the filling.

sicilian stuffed tuna rolls
Prepare the basic recipe, replacing the swordfish with thin slices of tuna.

sicilian stuffed plaice rolls
Prepare the basic recipe, replacing the swordfish with evenly trimmed plaice (flounder) fillets. Bear in mind that the plaice will be more delicate than the swordfish and will cook more quickly.

grilled shrimp with citrus aïoli

see base recipe page 240

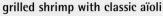

grilled shrimp with classic aïoli
Prepare the basic recipe, replacing all the citrus zest in the aïoli with 2 extra cloves minced garlic and 1 heaped tablespoon of finely chopped fresh flat-leaf parsley.

grilled shrimp with pesto mayonnaise
Prepare the basic recipe, replacing all the citrus zest and garlic in the aïoli with 1 heaping tablespoon pesto.

grilled shrimp with herbed mayonnaise
Prepare the basic recipe, replacing all the citrus zest in the aïoli with 3 tablespoons finely chopped fresh mixed herbs, stirred into the mayonnaise with the minced garlic.

grilled shrimp and squid with citrus aïoli
Prepare the basic recipe, replacing half the shrimp with cleaned baby squid.

variations

steamed mussels with pesto

see base recipe page 241

steamed mussels with white wine, shallots & garlic
Steam the mussels according to the basic recipe, and omit the pesto. Simply serve the steamed mussels with crusty bread.

spicy steamed mussels
Prepare the basic recipe, omitting the pesto. Add 1 teaspoon crushed red chile pepper to the steaming liquid to add fire to the whole dish.

steamed mussels with couscous
Prepare the basic recipe. Strain the liquid from the mussels before mixing with the pesto, and use the liquid (about 1 3/4 cups—make up the quantity with extra hot water or fish stock) to pour over a scant 1/2 pound couscous. Cover and steam until cooked, fluff with a fork, and use as the base for the mussels, mixed with the pesto, instead of crusty bread.

steamed mussels with pesto & butter beans
Prepare the basic recipe, replacing the tomatoes with 1 (14-oz.) can of butter beans, drained, then stirred into the pesto.

variations

baked stuffed baby squid on a bed of fennel

see base recipe page 242

baked stuffed baby squid with olive filling
Prepare the basic recipe, replacing the chorizo and feta filling with a filling
made from soft bread crumbs mixed with chopped garlic, chopped mint,
chopped green pitted olives, a little olive oil, salt, and pepper.

baked stuffed baby squid on a bed of potatoes
Prepare the basic recipe, replacing the boiled fennel with a bed of boiled
new potatoes, thickly sliced and dressed with a little olive oil and freshly
ground black pepper.

spicy baked stuffed baby squid
Prepare the basic recipe, adding 1 teaspoon chili powder to the feta and
chorizo filling mixture.

baked stuffed baby squid with a potato filling
Prepare the basic recipe, replacing the filling with a mixture of mashed
potatoes, 2 tablespoons crumbled feta or goat's cheese, oregano, minced
garlic, salt, pepper, and olive oil.

fish & seafood   253

variations

sea bass in salt crust

see base recipe page 244

sea bream in salt crust
Prepare the basic recipe, replacing the sea bass with sea bream.

salmon in salt crust
Prepare the basic recipe, replacing the sea bass with salmon.

sea bass in salt crust with herbs
Prepare the basic recipe, adding a large handful of chopped fresh mixed herbs to the salt and egg white mixture before spreading it over the fish.

sea bass in salt crust with lemon zest
Prepare the basic recipe, adding the grated zest of 2 lemons to the salt and egg white mixture before spreading it over the fish.

crisp shrimp fritters

see base recipe page 246

crisp squid fritters
Prepare basic recipe, replacing shrimp with small squid, boiled until tender, drained, and well dried before chopping. Replace the cup of shrimp cooking water with 1 cup of squid cooking water.

crisp mussel fritters
Prepare basic recipe, replacing shrimp with very large, steamed mussels, shelled and well drained before chopping. Replace the cup of shrimp cooking water with 1 cup of mussel cooking liquid.

crisp cod fritters
Prepare basic recipe, replacing shrimp with cubes of cod, lightly poached and well drained before chopping. Replace the cup of shrimp cooking water with 1 cup of cod poaching water.

crisp scallop fritters
Prepare basic recipe, replacing shrimp with clean, medium-sized scallops, lightly seared in a little oil before chopping, chilling, and coating with the batter. In this case, because the scallops are not poached, use tap water for thinning the batter.

fruit & desserts

In hot weather, imaginative, refreshing, yet

nourishing fruit and desserts are an absolute must.

This chapter contains many of the classic desserts,

as well as some more unusual examples of fruits

and desserts prepared in many of the Mediterranean

countries during the hot summer, when fresh

produce is at its very best.

lemon granita

see variations page 272

This is like a very simple lemon sorbet, only much more gritty and granular. It is very refreshing and can help you feel a lot less full after a very big, heavy meal. In Italy (where it is called *granita di limone*) this would be eaten either as a light dessert, or just to help you cool off. It's also delicious with a mixed citrus fruit salad.

1 quart cold water
1 generous cup sugar
1 cup freshly squeezed lemon juice

In a saucepan, heat 1/4 cup of the water with all the sugar. Bring it to a boil and cook long enough to dissolve all the sugar. Allow sugar syrup to cool, then add the remaining water and lemon juice. Stir well and pour into a shallow aluminum pan (a cake pan is perfect). Place pan in the freezer.

Remove from the freezer after half an hour and scrape down the sides and bottom of the pan, breaking up the part that has solidified, and blending it into the part that is still liquid. Repeat this every half hour, until the granita has become a fairly firm, flaky slush. At this point, remove it from the pan and ideally serve at once. If you are not eating it immediately, transfer it to a sealable plastic container and return to the freezer. If you leave it too long in the metal container, it will "burn" (the water will separate and form ice crystals).

Serves 8–10

orange salad with almonds

see variations page 273

This very light, cleansing salad is the perfect dessert to serve at the end of a long and heavy meal. It looks especially dramatic when prepared with blood oranges.

10 large oranges
4 tbsp. slivered almonds
vanilla ice cream or crème fraîche, to serve

amaretti cookies or toasted slivered almonds,
to serve

Peel 9 of the oranges carefully, removing all the pith. Slice them into neat segments or rounds, removing any seeds. Put them in a large bowl. Toast the almonds briefly in a hot skillet until just golden and scented. Add the almonds to the oranges and mix. Serve now or refrigerate until ready to serve. Slice the remaining orange into thin segments. Serve the salad with vanilla ice cream or crème fraîche, orange segments, and a few crumbled or whole amaretti cookies or toasted, slivered almonds on top.

Serves 6

egyptian sweet couscous

see variations page 274

Among the variations of couscous, this recipe from Egypt is unrivaled for the sweet-toothed palate. It's traditionally served with a cold glass of milk or a cup of heavy Arabic coffee.

2 cups fruit juice, strawberry, raspberry,
   blueberry, or cranberry
2 tbsp. rose water
1 cup couscous
3 tbsp. melted sweet butter

1/4 cup almond meal
1/4 cup finely ground pistachios
1/2 cup confectioners' sugar
1/2–1 tbsp. ground cinnamon
1/2 cup pomegranate seeds

In a saucepan, bring fruit juice and rose water to a boil. Add couscous, stir well, cover, remove from heat, and let stand 15 minutes. Fluff with a fork. Rub melted butter into the grains thoroughly. Mix in the almond meal and pistachios.

Mound on a serving platter and sprinkle with mixture of confectioners' sugar and cinnamon. Serve at room temperature. Garnish with pomegranate seeds.

Serves 6

baklava

see variations page 275

It is important that the nuts used for making this classic dessert from Turkey and Greece are as fresh as possible for the best results. Also, the honey should be thick and tasty.

1 lb. chopped walnuts
1 tsp. ground cinnamon
1 (16-oz.) package phyllo dough
1 cup unsalted butter, melted

1 cup granulated sugar
1 cup water
1 tsp. pure vanilla extract
1/2 cup honey

Preheat oven to 350°F. Butter the bottoms and sides of a 9x13-inch baking pan. Toss walnuts with cinnamon and set aside. Unroll phyllo dough. Cut whole stack in half to fit pan. Cover phyllo with a dampened cloth to keep it from drying as you work. Place 2 sheets of dough in pan and brush thoroughly with melted butter. Repeat with another layer of 2 sheets to create a thick base. Sprinkle 2–3 tablespoons of nut mixture on top. Top with 2 sheets of dough, spread with butter, sprinkle with nuts, and top with 2 sheets of dough. Keep building layers until you have filled the pan.

Using a sharp knife, cut into diamonds or squares all the way to the bottom of the pan. You may cut into 4 long rows, then make diagonal cuts. Bake for about 50 minutes until baklava is golden and crisp. While baklava is baking, boil sugar and water until sugar is melted. Add vanilla and honey. Simmer for about 20 minutes until sauce is thickened. Remove baklava from oven and immediately spoon sauce over it. Let cool. Leave it uncovered, because it gets soggy if it is wrapped. Eat on the same day, or cover with a clean cloth and use the next day, though it will keep well for 3 or 4 days.

Serves 6

catalan cream

see variations page 276

Crema catalana is the Catalan version of the French dessert, *crème brulée*. In fact, many regions lay claim to the origin of the dessert. It is also called *Crema de Sant Josep*, or St. Joseph's Cream, traditionally prepared on March 19, St. Joseph's Day, the Spanish equivalent of Father's Day in the U.S.

4 egg yolks	grated zest of 1 lemon
1 cup superfine sugar	2 cups milk
1 stick cinnamon	1 tbsp. cornstarch

In a saucepan, beat together the egg yolks and 3/4 cup of the sugar until thoroughly blended and the mixture turns frothy. Add the cinnamon stick and grated lemon zest. Pour in the milk and cornstarch. Slowly heat the mixture, stirring constantly, just until thickened. Remove from heat immediately. Remove the cinnamon stick and ladle the milk mixture into 4–6 ramekins (depending on size). Allow to cool, then refrigerate for at least 2–3 hours.

Before serving, preheat the broiler. Remove ramekins from refrigerator and sprinkle evenly with the remaining sugar. When the broiler is hot, put the ramekins under the broiler and allow the sugar to caramelize, turning gold and brown. This may take 10 minutes or so, depending on the heat. Watch them very carefully and remove as soon as they're the right color. Serve immediately.

If you like, you can serve the dessert chilled, but it has more flavor when served warm from the broiler and the caramel will melt after refrigeration.

Serves 4–6

almond ice cream

see variations page 277

Cooling ice creams made with nuts such as pistachios, hazelnuts, and almonds are very popular all over the Mediterranean. You can also buy creamy almond milk in cartons in some Middle Eastern stores, which will make this whole recipe much faster.

1/4 cup blanched almonds
2 cups whole milk
3/4 cup heavy cream

3 egg yolks
1/2 cup superfine sugar
1 teaspoon kirsch (or liqueur of your choice)

Pound the almonds into a paste. Add milk and heavy cream and mix thoroughly together. Pour the almond mixture into a saucepan and bring it to a boil. Remove from heat and allow to cool.

In a separate bowl, mix egg yolks, sugar, and kirsch for 5 minutes. Slowly pour the cooled almond milk into the yolks and mix well with a wooden spoon. Return the mixture to a low heat for 5 minutes, stirring constantly and without letting it boil. Remove from the heat and allow to cool again. Strain it carefully through a sieve into an ice cream maker and freeze until the ice cream is very firm. If you do not have an ice cream maker, pour the mixture into a plastic container with a lid and place it in the freezer. Mix well with a fork every hour, or when the edges of the ice cream are beginning to solidify, until the ice cream is set and crystal-free.

Serves 4

watermelon & feta salad

see variations page 278

If you're someone who likes combining the flavors of sweet and salty, the combination of watermelon and feta is just for you. It's so simple, yet so fabulous.

2 large slices watermelon
1/4 lb. feta cheese, crumbled
5–6 leaves fresh mint

Remove the seeds from the watermelon and cut the flesh into chunks or scoop into balls. Arrange these on a dish or in a bowl and sprinkle the crumbled feta cheese over them. Chop the mint finely and scatter over the dish to serve. If you wish to make the recipe ahead, chill the prepared watermelon until required, then add the feta and mint just before serving.

Serves 4

cinnamon frost

see variations page 279

Called *gelo di cannella* in Sicily, this is a very light dessert, perfect to serve at the end of a long and spicy meal. The flavor of cinnamon is incredibly intense and surprisingly refreshing. Please be aware that the cinnamon sticks need to infuse in the water for a very long time, so start this dessert the day before you need it.

4 cinnamon sticks
3 1/4 cups cold water
1 1/2 cups sugar
2 1/2 oz. cornstarch

2 (1-oz.) squares baking chocolate
ground cinnamon and grated chocolate,
    to decorate

Put the cinnamon sticks and cold water into a saucepan. Set it over medium heat and bring to a boil, then boil gently for about 5 minutes. Remove from the heat and let stand to infuse for 12 hours. Strain the cinnamon liquid carefully and return to the pan. Discard cinnamon sticks. Add the sugar to the cinnamon liquid. Dissolve the cornstarch in 2 tablespoons of the liquid, then add the thickened liquid to the pan. Bring to a boil, stirring constantly, and boil very gently until thickened. Remove from the heat and add the chocolate. Stir until the chocolate has melted. Turn into 1 large or 6 small individual molds and chill until solid. Turn out to serve, decorated with cinnamon and grated chocolate.

Serves 6

flan

see variations page 280

This very rich and creamy Spanish baked custard is very easy to make. It is lovely served with a fruit compote.

1 cup granulated sugar	1 (12-oz.) can evaporated milk
3 extra-large eggs	1 tbsp. pure vanilla extract
1 (14-oz.) can sweetened condensed milk	

Preheat oven to 350ºF. In a medium saucepan over medium-low heat, melt sugar until liquified and golden in color. Carefully pour hot syrup into a 9-inch round baking dish, turning the dish to evenly coat the bottom and sides. Set aside.

In a large bowl, beat eggs. Beat in condensed milk, evaporated milk, and vanilla until smooth. Pour mixture into baking dish. Cover with aluminum foil. Bake in preheated oven for 60 minutes. Let cool completely. To serve, carefully invert cool flan on serving plate.

Serves 6–8

cream cheese mint tart

see variations page 281

Flaó is similar to American cheesecake, but the use of mint leaves in the filling and the anisette and anise seeds in the pastry sets it apart and makes it particularly refreshing. It calls for *requesón*, a Spanish fresh milk cheese, although any ordinary cream cheese will also work.

For the pastry
3 tbsp. olive oil
3 tbsp. lard, at room temperature
6 tbsp. water
2 tbsp. anisette liqueur or sambuca (optional)
1 tbsp. anise seeds
1 cup all-purpose flour, plus extra for dusting
1 tbsp. granulated sugar
pinch salt

For the filling
9 fresh mint leaves
1 tbsp. grated lemon zest
1/3 cup sugar
1 cup (8 oz.) cream cheese, at room temperature
2 eggs
juice of 1/2 lemon
2 tbsp. confectioners' sugar, for dusting

Preheat the oven to 400°F.

To make the pastry, combine all the ingredients, and stir with a wooden spoon until they form a rough dough. Turn the dough onto a lightly floured work surface and knead for about 10 minutes, or until soft and no longer sticky. Clean the work surface, dust again with flour, and roll out the dough into a thin round at least 13 inches in diameter.

Carefully transfer the dough round to a 10-inch springform pan with 2-inch sides, pressing it into the bottom and sides. Trim away the excess dough.

Serves 6

To make the filling, combine 3 of the mint leaves, lemon zest, and sugar in a blender or food processor, and process on high speed until fine. Add cream cheese, eggs, and lemon juice, and process until smooth. Pour the mixture into the prepared crust. Bake the tart for 30 minutes, or until set when tested with a knife in the center. Transfer to a wire rack and let cool in the pan. Remove the pan sides and slide the tart onto a flat serving plate. Garnish with the remaining mint leaves and dust with confectioners' sugar. Serve at room temperature.

variations

lemon granita

see base recipe page 257

coffee granita
Prepare the basic recipe, replacing the lemon juice with a cup of very strong espresso. The classic coffee granita is perfect served with a topping of whipped cream.

watermelon granita
Prepare the basic recipe, replacing the lemon juice with the thick, pulpy juice of watermelon. Adjust the sugar content accordingly by tasting the mixture before freezing.

orange granita
Prepare the basic recipe, replacing the lemon juice with orange juice and adjusting the sugar content accordingly (the orange juice is not so sour).

lime granita
Prepare the basic recipe, replacing the lemon juice with fresh lime juice.

orange salad with almonds

see base recipe page 258

orange salad with pistachios
Prepare the basic recipe, replacing the almonds with coarsely chopped pistachios.

orange salad with walnuts
Prepare the basic recipe, replacing the almonds with chopped walnuts.

orange & pink grapefruit salad
Prepare the basic recipe, replacing 4 of the oranges with 3 pink grapefruit.

orange salad with almonds & pomegranate seeds
Prepare the basic recipe, adding a handful of pomegranate seeds to the oranges before adding the almonds.

orange salad with grand marnier
Prepare the basic recipe, adding some Grand Marnier or other orange-flavored liqueur over the oranges before mixing in the almonds.

variations

egyptian sweet couscous

see base recipe page 261

sweet couscous with candied almonds
Prepare the basic recipe, then garnish with candied (Jordan) almonds, scattered over the top.

sweet couscous with candied citrus
Prepare the basic recipe, replacing the rose water with orange blossom water, and adding 3 tablespoons finely chopped candied orange to the nuts.

sweet couscous with fruit compôte
Prepare the basic recipe, then serve it with a little warm mixed fruit compôte.

sweet couscous with candied pineapple
Prepare the basic recipe, adding cubes of candied pineapple to the cooked couscous before adding the rest of the ingredients.

baklava

see base recipe page 262

baklava with pistachios
Prepare the basic recipe, replacing the walnuts with coarsely chopped pistachios.

baklava with chocolate
Prepare the basic recipe, adding a layer of melted bittersweet chocolate by drizzling it between each phyllo pastry layer with the nuts and honey.

baklava with almonds
Prepare the basic recipe, replacing the walnuts with a mixture of ground and slivered almonds and almond meal.

baklava with mixed nuts
Prepare the basic recipe, replacing the walnuts with a combination of coarsely chopped pistachios, almonds, and walnuts.

catalan cream

see base recipe page 264

catalan cream with nutmeg
Prepare the basic recipe, replacing the cinnamon stick with 1/4 teaspoon freshly grated nutmeg.

catalan cream with orange & lemon
Prepare the basic recipe, replacing the cinnamon stick with a 3-inch strip of lemon peel, left whole, from 1 lemon. Replace the grated lemon zest with the grated zest of 1/2 orange.

vanilla catalan cream
Prepare the basic recipe, replacing the cinnamon stick and lemon zest with the seeds removed from 1 whole vanilla pod.

catalan cream with pistachios
Prepare the basic recipe, then add 2 tablespoons finely ground pistachios into the mixture while it is still warm, just before pouring into the ramekins for cooling and setting.

chocolate catalan cream
Prepare the basic recipe, replacing the lemon zest and cinnamon with 1 heaping tablespoon unsweetened cocoa powder.

variations

almond ice cream

see base recipe page 265

almond & pistachio ice cream
Prepare the basic recipe, then before freezing add a handful of chopped pistachios for a crunchy texture.

almond & pine nut ice cream
Prepare the basic recipe, using 1/8 cup almonds and 1/8 cup pine nuts.

almond & hazelnut ice cream
Prepare the basic recipe, using 1/8 cup almonds and 1/8 cup skinned hazelnuts (toast them briefly in the oven, then wrap in a clean cloth while still warm and rub vigorously to remove the skins).

almond & raisin ice cream
Prepare the basic recipe, adding 3 tablespoons raisins, soaked in kirsch, to the mixture just before freezing.

almond & amaretto ice cream
Prepare the basic recipe, replacing the kirsch with 1 tablespoon amaretto liqueur and 4 crumbled amaretti cookies. Bear in mind that the extra alcohol in the amaretto will prevent the ice cream from becoming entirely solid.

variations

watermelon & feta salad

see base recipe page 267

cantaloupe & feta salad
Prepare the basic recipe, replacing the watermelon with 1 small cantaloupe.

honeydew melon, watermelon & feta salad
Prepare the basic recipe, replacing the watermelon with a combination of
watermelon and honeydew melon.

watermelon, chile pepper & feta salad
Prepare the basic recipe, then to add a little spice, sprinkle 1/2 or 1/4 fresh
chile pepper, very finely chopped, over the watermelon with the feta
and mint.

watermelon, feta & chervil salad
Prepare the basic recipe, replacing the mint with finely chopped chervil for a
more delicate flavor.

watermelon, feta & pistachio salad
Prepare the basic recipe, replacing the mint with 2 tablespoons
chopped pistachios.

cinnamon frost

see base recipe page 268

clear cinnamon frost
If you prefer a clearer finish, replace the cornstarch with unflavored gelatin (follow instructions on the package). In this case, you will add the gelatin to the liquid once you have strained it and returned it to a boil.

cinnamon frost with lemon
Prepare the basic recipe, adding 1 teaspoon fresh lemon juice and 1 teaspoon grated lemon zest to the mixture to give the frost a light lemony flavor.

cinnamon & clove frost
Prepare the basic recipe, adding 2 whole cloves to the water to infuse with the cinnamon.

cinnamon frost with melon salad
Prepare the basic recipe. Serve the cinnamon frost, cut into small cubes once set, over a salad of cubed, chilled fresh melon.

cinnamon & ginger frost
Prepare the basic recipe, adding 1/2 teaspoon ground ginger or a small knob of fresh ginger, grated, to the water to infuse with the cinnamon.

variations

flan

see base recipe page 269

flan with lemon
Prepare the basic recipe, replacing the vanilla extract with the very finely grated zest of 1/2 lemon.

flan with orange
Prepare the basic recipe, replacing the vanilla extract with the very finely grated zest of 1 orange.

flan with lime
Prepare the basic recipe, replacing the vanilla extract with the very finely grated zest of 1 lime.

flan with nutmeg
Prepare the basic recipe, replacing the vanilla extract with 1/4 teaspoon freshly grated nutmeg.

flan with cinnamon
Prepare the basic recipe, replacing the vanilla extract with 1/4 teaspoon ground cinnamon.

cream cheese mint tart

see base recipe page 270

cream cheese lemon tart
Make the basic pastry, replacing the anise seeds and liqueur with the grated zest of 1 lemon and 1 teaspoon lemon juice. Make the basic filling, omitting the mint. Garnish with thin slices of lemon.

cream cheese orange tart
Make the basic pastry, replacing the anise seeds and liqueur with the grated zest of 1 orange and 1 teaspoon orange juice. Make the basic filling, omitting the mint and replacing the lemon zest and juice with orange zest and juice and garnishing with thin slices of orange.

cream cheese basil tart
Prepare the basic recipe, replacing the mint leaves with fresh basil for a very different taste. Omit the anise seeds.

cream cheese tarragon tart
Prepare the basic recipe, replacing the mint leaves with the same quantity of fresh tarragon leaves for a more intense flavor.

index